Praise For Military Money

"Military Money is a compendium covering a wide range of financial topics specific to the military Service Member but applicable to almost everyone. It is written in a witty and engaging style, with anecdotes and examples used to illustrate otherwise complex concepts. Trevor's Military Money challenges conventional 'barracks' wisdom and, instead, is a comprehensive and entertaining guide for anyone looking to improve their financial fitness.

If you're looking for a book with a prescriptive, A-to-Z checklist on how to make your money work for you, this is not the book for you and the reality, there is no single book for you because every person and every situation is uniquely different. What you will find is an outstanding resource with recommendations to begin or advance your journey to financial freedom . Military

Money is written as a concise, understandable, easily-digestible reference with practical tools and tips for readers to apply the techniques in their own lives.

I thoroughly enjoyed reading Military Money and picked up many strategies to apply moving forward, and I'm confident you will too!"

Lt Col Adrian Cercenia, USSF, Retired

"Trevor delivers a straightforward, educational approach to building a strong financial strategy, discipline, and independence for those serving our nation. I only wish I had this kind of advice in my early years."

CAPT Erik Thors, USN, Retired

"I really wish Trevor would have written this back in 2002 when I first came into the military! I really could have used it!"

MSgt Chris Vanwy, USAF, Retired

PRAISE FOR MILITARY MONEY

"How I wish I had this book when I first put the uniform on. This is a treasure chest of knowledge that will arm Service Members, irrespective of where they are in their careers, with information and tips on how to thrive on a monthly government salary. It grabs you in the preface and provides a roadmap to success. Learn from a savvy financial guru who learned many hard lessons; now he wants to make sure other Service Members don't repeat his mistakes."

LTC Carl "Chip" Frazer USA, Retired

"I have known Trevor for 18 years, and I have always been impressed with his financial prowess. As you will learn by reading this book, he has made mistakes, but through desire and discipline, he has more than recovered. In fact, his financial success is the absolute envy of many of his friends and mentors because he is truly financially independent. That is, he is able to do what he wants, when he wants, and with who he wants - a goal out of reach of most of his peers who have retired from the military or government service."

Col Monte T. Muñoz, USAF, Retired

MILITARY MONEY

HOW TO THRIVE ON A GOVERNMENT SALARY

TREVOR C. NOLAN, USAF, RETIRED

WITH MICHAEL MRAS, USAF, RETIRED

MILITARY MIGHT PUBLISHING

Library of Congress Control Number: 2023907932

ISBN: 978-1-961019-00-3
E-book ISBN: 978-1-961019-01-0

Printed in the United States of America

www.militarymightpublishing.com

"The best way to predict the future is to create it."

~ Peter Drucker

Contents

Dedication

To my family for inspiring in me a servant's heart.
and
To every Soldier, Sailor, Airman, Marine, Guardian, and
Coastguardsmen that have and continues to serve.
This book is for you.

Foreword

When I initially met the author of Military Money, the first thing I noticed, after his big contagious smile, was that he radiated trust. Perhaps it was so apparent because of the lack of trust in our world today. Regardless, Trevor Nolan leans into relationships with so much assurance that you just know you can rely on his absolute authenticity. He will be the first one to tell you this quality has gotten him burned in the past, yet he continues to extend it without hesitation. That's why he is the perfect person to write this book, which is essentially a primer Service Members can use to help them navigate a multitude of important financial decisions during their military career. A retired Service Member himself, the author of this book is the type of person I would want as my shipmate, wingman, or whatever your branch of service calls the military brother and sister who is watching out for your best interest. His character, coupled with his intelligence and broad range of experiences, makes Military Money a "how-to" manual every Service Member can benefit from reading.

Each person who serves in the military pledges an oath and makes a sacrifice in serving their country. Whether being stationed in a far-off land, putting their lives on the line, or simply being away from family and loved ones, the men and women who serve in America's armed forces deserve our utmost respect and gratitude. Yet, despite their sacrifice and service, many Military Members struggle to make sound financial decisions. This is due to numerous reasons, such as lack of financial education, the stress of deployment, and simply the demands of military life. The fact is that too many of our brave servicemen and women find themselves struggling with debt, living paycheck to paycheck, and uncertain about their financial future. That's why this book is so important. By providing practical, actionable advice drawn from both the author's personal experiences as well as from available research, this book aims to help Military Members make better financial decisions and achieve greater financial security. It offers a wealth of insights, tips, and strategies to help Military Members build a strong financial foundation and achieve their long-term financial goals. As a society, we owe it to our Military Members to provide them with the tools they need to succeed not just on the battlefield, but also in their financial lives. I'm confident that this book will be an invaluable resource for anyone serving in the military, as well as their families, and I'm honored to contribute to it.

I think most of us actually grow up and learn to be adults through our experiences in the military. From the moment we set foot on the ground at basic training, until we separate from the military, we are faced with choices which invariably affect our outcomes in life. We are mature enough to fight for our country, and ready or not, we also begin to bear the responsibility of making lots of important decisions. Moreover, the decisions we make have an enduring impact on our dependents and loved ones as well. The importance of financial literacy cannot be overstated, especially for those in the military. While this book may not be an exhaustive list encompassing every situation, I believe it focuses on the key issues facing members of the armed forces from a financial perspective.

In my career as a financial planner and retirement planning counselor, the best part of my job is getting to have meaningful conversations with my clients. I view it as my responsibility to positively impact their financial lives. Financial wellness contributes significantly to overall wellness. The process starts by understanding their personal and financial circumstances thoroughly. Then we identify and select goals for their financial future, which includes discussing their goals, dreams, and even fears. I will analyze the current course of action against alternative courses of action, develop my recommendations, and then present the recommendations to the client. Once they choose the desired course of action, we then implement the plan they have selected. Finally, we resolve to monitor the plan and to make changes where needed.

I strive to have a personal relationship with each and every person, and it is truly my privilege to walk with men and women who have attained this level in life. Often, we laugh, and occasionally we cry, but I always try to listen to the wisdom behind their stories. I see retirement as the product of one's life, the culmination of 60+ years of life choices, victories, defeats, and circumstances. In the best cases, I help people live out their retirement years with dignity and comfort. We talk about optimizing withdrawals from their retirement account, as well as what kind of legacy they want to leave behind when they're gone. I learn about their grandchildren, what causes they support, and how they spend their leisure time. This is the ideal situation, but it is certainly not the case with every situation.

I also meet with people in or near retirement who are struggling. These conversations are the most challenging, because as you near the finish line there are very few hypothetical levers you can pull to change your situation. For many, it is not a matter of how they will distribute their assets when they pass away, but instead the concern is whether they have enough to actually support themselves through retirement. Earning more money is no longer an option, and spending less means having to choose between medicine and food. It's heartbreaking, but often it is also avoidable. I frequently hear that the key to success is in avoiding too many mistakes. While one need not live in fear of making mistakes, I believe preventing unforced errors is the surest path to winning.

By following his advice prescribed in this book, Trevor Nolan aims to help the amazing servicemen and women of this country achieve success. Heroes, take note of the many nuggets of wisdom to be found in this book. Your future self will thank you.

Brandon Ridenour, CRPC®
Wealth Manager - Kassira Wealth Management LLC
Mobile: 719-477-3132
Website: Kassira.com

Brandon Ridenour, CRPC® is a veteran of the US Coast Guard, and is a financial planner and retirement planning counselor.

Acknowledgments

No one achieves goals on their own. It takes family, friends, and mentors to truly achieve a lasting impact. If wealth can be measured by those surrounding you and supporting you, I am very wealthy. I must thank my family, that helped me on this path after my military retirement. To my grandfather, who inspired me to join the Air Force; my grandmother for raising me; my mother for demonstrating that learning never ends; and all my aunts, uncles, and cousins who keep me humble and lift me up.

Special thanks to my aunt and business partner in all things, Joanne, for her constant support, to my cousin, Candace, for help with the cover and every emergency editing project, and to Aspen and Ryker for your patience and love.

To those that helped by providing feedback, editing, and testimonials, Adrian "Ace" Cercenia, Carl "Chip" Frazer, Monte

"Zooma" Muñoz, Brian Swanson, Erik "Blue" Thors, Chris "Space Unicorn" Vanwy, thank you all for making Military Money a valuable resource. I also want to express my deepest gratitude to Brandon Ridenour for his kind and thoughtful foreword. Brandon's heart is in this mission. He works daily to improve the financial literacy and quality of life of our active duty members and Veterans.

Lastly, to my often-overlooked wingman and fellow Veteran, Michael. Thank you for sincerely caring about this project and for your time, talent, and sage advice. You have given a voice to so many, including me.

Preface

Being broke sucks. The promise of being rich is awesome. Buy a lottery ticket and you buy yourself a dream. I'm here to say the dream can be real, and you don't have to win the lottery. You have everything you need right now to make it all a reality. This book is a resource intended for YOU. You will be faced with difficult and hugely impactful financial decisions at every point in your career. From the day you raise your right hand and swear the oath to support and defend the Constitution of the United States to the day you leave your last duty station, Military Money will detail how you can thrive on a government salary. As a retired military member, I made some good, and many poor financial decisions. Over my years on active duty, I met some folks who made far worse and far better financial decisions. I captured the wins and losses in this book so that you can reap the benefits and avoid the pitfalls.

The good news is that you do not need to follow every suggested tactic in this book. That would be amazing and reap the highest rewards, but it wouldn't be much fun. Personally, I have always been a 'live life to the fullest' kind of guy. In that vein, I spend my money to make experiences more than chasing the shiniest material items. Ultimately, it doesn't matter if you are a spender or a saver; the tips in this book will arm you with valuable knowledge that you can turn into positive action.

Your time in service, whether four, ten, fifteen, or twenty-plus years, offers you something your civilian peers can truly envy: scheduled pay raises and nearly assured promotions. The security of a military paycheck, twice a month, for as long as you serve, allows you to aggressively save and grow wealth, unlike any other profession. Military Money is filled with strategies, tactics, and hacks that will independently and cooperatively lead to personal wealth for the day you hang up the uniform for good. I have put these suggestions together by stealing every good idea from my mentors, years of personal budgeting, and trial and error. Now that I have retired from the Air Force, I have been called to help our active duty military and our Veterans. This book is the first offering of many that are aimed to help you succeed in everything you face in today's military and beyond.

This book is different from others because it is written with the military mind and heart at its core. The arguments you will have with your significant other, spouse, kid, or education office advisor are the same fights I have had. They're the same ones your peers have had, and it's time to take control and apply the lessons we collectively learned. It's time to arm you, individually, with the information you need to be successful. I want you to be able to do anything in this life you are called to after your military service, even if that is growing your hair long to donate to paint brush factories or raising goats to work in yoga studios.

"When you truly believe in what you are doing, it shows. And it pays. Winners in life are those who are excited about where they're going."

~ Unknown

A 2018 study showed that military service has produced twenty-one billionaires, more than any single university.[i] Additionally, thousands of those who served in the military have become millionaires. The road to extreme wealth is not a classified secret. Planning and discipline will get you there. During your time in service, you will be faced with countless financial decisions. Military Money will highlight these decision points and let you know what you can expect based on what you choose. Unlike other financial self-help books that preach about paying for everything in cash or, conversely, using other people's money to get ahead in life, Military Money will give you, in clear terms, the benefits and downfalls of each decision you will be faced with while in the military.

Before you put on a uniform or laced up your boots for the first time, a recruiter sold you on all the benefits military service could offer you. The most common benefits used to lure potential recruits are money for college, learning a marketable skill, and the promise to see the world. I'd be interested in how many of those recruiters told you that serving in the military will put you on a road that could lead to your future millionaire life.

My friend Michael (researcher for this book) and I have taken the time to select the most frequently faced financial decisions you will encounter while on active duty and explained how your decisions can lead to financial success. We describe personal assets and liabilities as the two critical components of your personal finances. Put simply, this book will turn you toward securing assets, those things you own or control that build your wealth.

"Your future self is being defined by the decisions you make today."

~Trevor Nolan

Conversely, liabilities are debts or obligations that you owe to someone else. Liabilities include mortgages, car loans, credit card debt, student loans, and other personal debts. From this point forward, the goal will be to minimize these liabilities.

The military is unlike any other workplace, there is true financial equality. It doesn't matter your gender, race, religion, color, or creed. You have the tools at your disposal right now to become a wealthy individual. Don't worry; this will not come at the expense of personal enjoyment. There will be plenty of money available for you to enjoy your life while serving in uniform. You do not have to live in poverty. Even if money is tight right now, this book will provide you with resources and ideas to get you working in the right direction.

The following chapters are bite-sized and should only take a few minutes of your time to consume. Don't feel like you need to read this book cover to cover. This is meant to be used as a resource you can rely on when faced with a financial decision. If a chapter doesn't apply to you, move on. Come back when and if you are faced with that situation in the future. Additionally, use the information from this book to help your friends in your unit. These tips, hacks, tactics, or whatever you want to call them, can be used by everyone, regardless of their time in.

Supporters and trolls will be ready to endorse or crush my recommendations throughout Military Money. Remember, this isn't prescriptive. I want you to be armed with the lessons I painfully learned along the way. I want nothing more than for every reader of this book to have accumulated wealth for their life after the military. If you like the book, the absolute best thing you can do for any author is to leave a positive review on Amazon. If you despise the book, I'd prefer you keep it our little secret.

This book is a call to action. I am excited for YOU and for all YOUR successes. The time to start is now. Let's roll.

1

Housing

"There is no place like home."

~ L. Frank Baum

In 2003, the movie *Old School* starring Vince Vaughn, Will Farrell, and Luke Wilson, came out. This movie was an instant hit for me and my friends, all in our early 20s, new in the military, and far from home. My roommate and I would watch it repeatedly. I don't know which of us liked it more. There is a scene in the movie where Blue, played by Patrick Cranshaw, has a birthday at a fraternity house. During this scene, his fraternity brothers host a wrestling match indoors in an inflatable pool filled with KY Jelly. At the time, my roommate and I were renting a home with a finished basement. I thought reenacting the *Old School* scene in our basement would be a great time. To this day, I don't regret it. Fast forward to today, I now have several properties with renters in them, and I can't say I'd be too hyped to find out that a party like that took place in one of my houses. We had a great time, but it ended up costing me half of the security deposit for deep cleaning. Despite the hit on my security deposit, I still saved a lot of money during that assignment by splitting housing costs with a roommate. Steve, if you or anyone else has pictures from that night, my contact info is in the back of the book.

Housing is the perfect place to start this book. Shelter is one of our most basic physiological needs (according to Maslow's Hierarchy of Needs).[ii] It's also where you will spend the majority of your military pay every month. As a service member, you will likely live on base and off base during your time in the military. On base housing can be broken down into barracks/dormitories or base housing (possibly contract housing). All these options remove basic allowance for housing (BAH) from your check in exchange for the keys to your very own (or shared) place to live close to work. Off base options will all come at your personal expense, and for your trouble, DFAS (Defense Finance & Accounting Service) will give you BAH based on your rank and dependent status. Your off base options run the spectrum. On one end, you could pitch a tent in a homeless camp and keep your expenses very low (looking at you infantry). On the other end of the scale, you could buy your own single-family home. In between those options, you could rent an entire place or a portion of a shared apartment, townhouse, condo, or house. Like many of you, I have tried every option on the scale depending on my duty assignment. Unfortunately, I was only intentional with my living arrangements toward the end of my career. With even an ounce of planning, I could have amassed a literal fortune simply by making better, deliberate decisions when it came to where I lived.

Suppose you are required to live in a dormitory/barracks. In that case, you can cash in on some huge advantages because although you aren't receiving BAH, you aren't spending money on miscellaneous household items and maintenance. The amount of money spent and re-spent on necessities like pots, pans, utensils, kitchen gadgets, etc., helps the stores around post stay in business but leaves you less money in your pocket. Believe me when I tell you when you opt to live off base, either to rent or to purchase, you will be required to repair some small item in your home almost every week—something you did not plan for. Not a day goes by when you must reach into your pocket to maintain, replace, or upgrade something that has malfunctioned in your home. In this chapter, I will describe the benefits and disadvantages of each living decision you could make. Then I'll leave you with a few ideas of how to save money while living on base or capitalizing on your tax-free BAH if you're living off base.

I will ask you a question to get you in the right frame of mind. Have you ever deliberately made your housing decision with long-term wealth generation in mind? My answer to this question was 'no' for nearly all of my assignments. If you ask yourself, 'How can I have access to as much money as I need now and still save for long-term wealth,' you will see large numbers in your balance sheet in just two assignments.

I want each of you to have the best quality of life now while planning for your future quality of life post-military. There are advantages and disadvantages to each decision you could make with respect to housing.

Housing Options and Variables

	Monthly Cost	Size	Noise	Maintenance	Commute	Insurance	Security	Privacy	Utilities
Barrack/Dorm	BAH	S	H	L	L	L	L	L	L
Room (Rent)	L	S	M	L	D	L	M	L	L
Apartment (Rent)	L	S	H	L	D	M	L	L	M
Condo (Buy)	L	S	H	M	D	H	L	L	M
Townhouse (Rent)	M	M	M	L	D	M	M	M	M
Townhouse (Buy)	M	M	L	H	D	H	M	M	M
House (On Base)	BAH	V	M	M	L	L	H	H	L
House (Rent)	H	V	L	L	D	M	H	M	H
House (Buy)	H	V	L	H	D	H	H	H	H

(H=High, M=Medium, L=Low, S=Small, D=Depends, V=Varies)

NEWS FLASH! When you are just starting in the military, you will not be able to (or shouldn't) afford a house like your parents.

Most people start out living in the dorms or in an apartment. This is a good choice for a couple of reasons since you can determine what you value (must haves) and what you can compromise on (nice to haves). The previous unscientific figure breaks down the available housing options and some variables you should consider when making your housing decision. **Pro Tip**: Moving during your assignment within the local area is hugely expensive and should only be done if absolutely necessary. So choose wisely!

Variables to consider when choosing your housing:

- **Cost:** On the surface, one of the most obvious ways to save money is selecting housing with a low monthly cost (at or below your BAH). Renting a room would be the cheapest option but at the expense of your privacy and personal space. If you live on base, at least you know that your monthly costs will remain constant and your maintenance costs will be very low. Renting an apartment, townhouse, or single family home may or may not be cheaper than buying. Still, your maintenance costs are lower, and moving out is much easier when you receive orders because you can automatically break your lease with no penalty. Buying a condo, townhouse, or single family home has the most considerable out-of-pocket costs (e.g., property tax and insurance), but you are building equity. Buying a home will likely be the most expensive thing you ever buy. Luckily, homeownership is considered an **asset**, meaning it has a very high probability of increasing in value after you buy it.

- **Size:** How much space do you actually need? Do you really 'need' an extra bedroom for your Pokémon Card collection? The size of dwellings varies across the United States. The national averages are below:

  - Apartment/Condo - 882 Sq Ft[iii]
  - Townhouse - 1750 Sq Ft[iv]
  - House - 2301 Sq Ft[v]

- **Noise Level:** The closer together people are, the noisier it is going to be. This might be fine if you are a heavy sleeper or work regular hours. However, if you are a light sleeper or have an alternative working schedule, this might play a much more significant role in your decision. Based on my experience, the thinner the walls, the nastier the neighbors.
- **Maintenance:** When living on base or renting, all major maintenance should be included. If you buy, you are responsible for all of it. Rooms, apartments, or condos should require no landscaping maintenance, while houses will have the most.
- **Commute:** If you live on base, your commute will be the shortest. Unfortunately, if your spouse or kids work off

base, they could face a long commute into town. Weather permitting, you might even be able to bike to work, which saves fuel, reduces vehicle maintenance costs, and gives you something to brag about at the office. Nice shorts, Lance.

- **Insurance:** If you live on base or rent, you should only need renter's insurance. However, if you buy, you must insure the property as well. This may include specialty insurance like fire or flood.
- **Security:** You can't beat the security you have living in an on-base house. Sadly, the dorms/barracks have more crime (mostly targets of opportunity in common areas). For every option, it depends on where you live. The suburbs tend to have the lowest crime rates but the highest costs. If you rent a room in a house, there is a greater chance someone will always be home. At the same time, everyone else in the house has access to your stuff. So, make sure you can trust them.
- **Privacy:** You will have the most privacy in your own home (shoutout to my friends at NSA). The one exception is if your neighborhood has an HOA (Homeowners Association). Just know that Karen will drive past your house and send nasty letters because your grass is too long, your plants are dead, or you are parked incorrectly. This is not unlike living on base, where there are lots of rules covering what you can and can't do.

- **Utilities:** On base, you typically don't pay (or pay very little) for essential utilities. Some utilities may have limitations, like water usage. If living off base, the larger your crib, the higher the utility bill will be each month.

Housing Options:

- **To Rent or To Own:** Renting may be the better option if you are not staying long, renting is cheaper than purchasing in your market, or your credit score is in the dumps. Owning property allows you to build long-term equity, and you can use the property to generate rental income when you move. This can be very lucrative. **Pro Tip**: The rental properties that generate the highest cash flow are often houses that cost below $200k. The exception would be a property used for short-term renters (e.g., Airbnb, VRBO), but those come with a greater investment in time and higher operating costs.
- If you use a VA or FHA loan to buy a property (discussed later), it is best to convert to a conventional mortgage when the property is no longer your primary residence. More on this tactic later in the book.
- **Fixer-Upper or New Build:** You might get a better price buying a fixer-upper, but you better have the time, money, and ability to do the repairs. Rehabbers and tradesmen are in high demand and can be difficult to

secure for smaller jobs. For a new build, there are a lot of additional costs you will need to consider (e.g., painting, window treatments, landscaping, fencing). Don't lie to yourself. Understand the true cost of the decision you are making.

Financing:

If you are going to buy. Know your budget before you start looking. Remember to factor in property taxes, insurance, HOA fees, etc. They may not be included in lender estimates as they vary wildly from location to location.

Pro Tip: Choose a lender and get pre-approved before you start looking. Many sellers require a pre-approval letter before you can place an offer on the house. Getting approved is simple as long as the property you find appraises for equal to or more than you are offering to pay. If not, rethink your decision. You can use websites like Nerdwallet and Zillow to help calculate your monthly payments.

- **Veteran's Administration (VA) Loan:** One of the best benefits you have as a current or former military member. With this loan, you can finance 100% of the value, meaning you do not have to put any money down. However, there are some restrictions with this loan type, as you can only have one at a time, and it must be your primary residence. For more information on VA Loans, go to https://www.benefits.va.gov/homeloans/

- **Federal Housing Administration (FHA)[vi] Loan:** The FHA - which is part of HUD (Housing and Urban Development)- insures the loan, so your lender can offer you a better deal. FHA is the largest insurer of residential mortgages in the world. FHA loan requirements and guidelines cover things like mortgage insurance, lending limits, debt-to-income ratios, credit issues, and closing costs. They also have special programs like the Good Neighbor Next Door program that your spouse may qualify for. It provides grants and housing discounts to teachers, officers, and firefighters. You can find more information at: https://www.hud.gov/program_offices /housing/sfh/reo/goodn/gnndabot. A list of general FHA qualification requirements is below:

  - FICO® score at least 580 = 3.5% down payment.
  - FICO® score between 500 and 579 = 10% down payment.
  - MIP (Mortgage Insurance Premium) is required.
  - Debt-to-Income Ratio < 43%.[vii] To calculate the debt-to-income ratio, divide your total monthly debt obligations (including rent or mortgage, student loan

payments, auto loan payments and credit card minimums) by your gross monthly income.
  - The home must be the borrower's primary residence.
  - The borrower must have a steady income and proof of employment.

- **Conventional Loan:**[viii] Conventional home loans have many advantages despite requiring a higher credit score and a higher down payment.

  - No Mortgage insurance is required with a 20% down payment.
  - Less strict appraisal standards.
  - Mortgage insurance can be eliminated at 80% LTV (Loan to Value). The loan-to-value (LTV) ratio is a measure comparing the amount of your mortgage with the appraised value of the property.[ix]
  - It can be used for investment property when you are relocated.
  - **Loan Terms:** Mortgages are highly customizable and should be examined with great care. As the purchaser/borrower, all responsibility falls on you once the deal is closed. Pay special attention to the following:
  - **15-Year vs. 30-Year Loans:** The interest rate is always lower on a 15-Year mortgage, saving you

money in the long run, but your monthly payments will be considerably higher. **Pro Tip**: Every 30-Year loan can be a 15-Year loan if you pay more monthly. The inverse is not true and will lead to foreclosure.

- **Fixed Rate vs. Adjustable Rate:**[x] A fixed-rate mortgage has an interest rate that won't change for the life of the loan. Adjustable-Rate Mortgages (ARMs) feature a fixed interest rate for a small period of time, typically three to ten years, and then fluctuate up or down for the subsequent years. ARMs generally are sought by people who plan on moving from (and selling) their houses within a few years.
- **Overpayment/Extra Payment:** Regardless of what loan you get, pay extra on your monthly mortgage if you can. Any additional money goes straight to the principal and will significantly reduce your loan period and the overall amount of interest paid. Always make sure there is not an early payoff penalty written into your mortgage. Depending on the total amount borrowed and your interest rate, one extra payment a year on a 30-year mortgage could take off as little as four but as many as nine years off your loan term and save you tens to hundreds of thousands on interest payments. You can do this by paying 1/12 extra monthly or saving up throughout the year to make a second payment in one month.[xi] Be sure to

write a note to your lender telling them of your intent to make a 'principal only' payment with the overpayment.

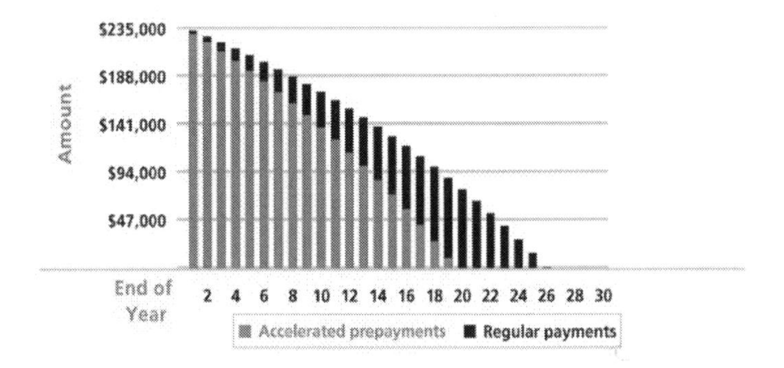

- **Refinance:** Refinancing your home can come with many upsides and few downsides while you are serving on active duty.

  - You could get a lower interest rate, saving you money in the long run. This could also reduce your monthly payment. Understand that although you reduce your monthly payment, you are extending the length of the loan and may end up paying more in the long run. Some exceptions like the IRRRL (Interest Rate Reduction Refinance Loan) may not reset your terms but adjust your interest rate in your favor.

- It is a way to take out some of the equity in your house to pay off some high-interest loans or cover emergency expenses.
- **Pro Tip**: Accessing additional cash through refinancing is a way to buy assets that can earn you a higher rate of return than your unrealized equity.
- **Property Taxes:** Always remember when something is going in your favor financially, the government will always take its cut. Property taxes can vary significantly from state to state (and sometimes, neighborhood by neighborhood). Some states may have special rules for military serving away from their home state of residence. Be sure to look at this expense before buying, this amount can greatly affect your monthly payment.
- **Rental Properties:** If you buy, you have the potential to rent out your property in part while you live there (called house hacking) or in whole once you move. This is a great way to make extra money. Make sure you have enough money saved to cover expenses when you don't have renters or need to make repairs.

Money Pits

- **Saving...but not saving...money:** It doesn't matter if you are able to save money on housing if you waste it on something else. Not saving/investing any money you've been able to keep from your monthly housing expenses is a fast track to staying poor.

- **Fixer-uppers:** This is literally where the term "Money Pit" comes from. For every problem you are aware of, many more are lurking. Ensure you have the money, time, ability, and diligence to keep up with the repairs.
- **Dead Beat Renters:** Make sure your tenants are well-vetted. If they stop paying, evicting them will be a lengthy process. This became a factor during COVID when people lost their jobs and were given protection from eviction. However, property owners were not protected from paying their mortgages. Be sure you have enough income to cover periods when your rental properties are not generating revenue.

2

Transportation

"The cars we drive say a lot about us."

~ Alexandra Paul

I am not a fan of stereotypes, especially when they are about people who choose to serve in the military. That said, I have personally embodied most of them. Look no further than my track record with transportation. I was the guy who showed up on active duty with a completely impractical, brand-new Yamaha R6 motorcycle because why wouldn't I? My parents cosigned on the loan, and I was cooler than Maverick in the first *Top Gun* (more on bad debt in chapter 13). The present me is wondering why in the world I thought that was the best time for me to be 'rolling' on two wheels when I had no idea where I would be headed after tech school. I am equally embarrassed and impressed with my youthful spirit and bravado.

Would you know it? During tech school, I discovered that I would be headed to Greenland after training for my first assignment. I was excited about the opportunity but quickly realized I had screwed myself with my poor financial decision. Since I couldn't take the motorcycle (or any personal vehicle) to Greenland, I placed it on the base 'lemon lot' and hoped for the best. After a few days another student offered to buy it from me. I was excited at the prospect that I dodged a bullet. I didn't want to have to make the payments and pay to store it for the year I was scheduled to be gone. With the promise that the check from the bank would be delivered to me by that Friday, I signed over the title and handed over the keys. I figured if I gave him possession right then and there he couldn't go back on the deal, and I was good to go. Friday came and went and then a second week passed, then another. I was starting to worry that my departure day would come, and I would have effectively given away a new motorcycle while still being responsible for the payments. I know,. I'm a dumbass. Lucky for me, everything was resolved in time...another narrow escape. In retrospect, did I allow those few weeks of sheer terror to engrain in me a life lesson so I would be smarter from then on? Of course not.

Fast forward to a little over two years later, I received a call from a nice gentleman informing me he was a Washington State Trooper in a town bordering Canada. I was confused because I was stationed in Colorado at the time. He was so kind to inform me that someone had abandoned a vehicle registered to me at a border crossing. I responded with, 'Are you sure?' He was, of course. I was standing there in my base house, feeling I had been duped. I took down the details of the impound lot and hung up. I was very newly divorced, like earlier that week. The car, a Honda Passport, was supposed to go with my ex and I would keep the pickup. Both vehicles had notes in my name. As we were going through our separation, I was told by my bank that she had been approved for a loan on the vehicle and would take over payments. Apparently, she never signed the loan documents, and I was now under the gun for two car notes.

To make matters worse, you have one week to vacate base housing when you get divorced. On top of that, I was on a crew schedule and worked nights. I'll spare you the details, but I never collected the impounded car. Instead, I focused on moving off base and spending all of my savings on a security deposit. (More on separation and divorce in Chapter 17). If I had the decision to do it over again, I would have gone to collect the vehicle and sold it. Instead, the bank recovered it and sold it at auction. I was forced to pay the difference in what I owed versus what they sold it for, the cost of the recovery, and the administration fees for selling it. To complete the full kick to my junk, the bank that held the loan considered it a repossession and reported it to every credit agency. It left a poop stain on my credit for years.

My third, and probably the most grotesque story about making terrible transportation decisions, would come ten or so years later when I got to Germany. I fell into the trap many of us do; I bought the fastest German car I could, with literally no reason to do so. Was it fun? Hell yes! Was it a complete money pit? Absolutely. The sticker price on the car was nearly $80K, but interest rates were at 0% at the time, which was great. I walked out without paying a single Euro in down payment and took on a car note of $950 a month for 84 months. To make matters worse, I spent thousands of additional Euros getting the car ceramic coated, the brake calipers powder coated, and the engine tuned. It was awesome and so freaking dumb.

This chapter will examine new vs. used cars and buying vs. leasing. We will also discuss toys that should almost always be rented versus purchased. Don't be me. It took me until 2019 to finally figure out how much money I wasted on vehicles.

In case you are wondering, I now own a 5-year-old diesel truck I bought used from a private seller and a small, 6-year-old SUV I also bought used from the original owner. Both are the highest optioned versions of those vehicles, and I am completely content with them. If I get the itch to drive a supercar, I rent one for the day.

Let's face it, functionally, vehicles are tools to get us from point A to point B. In reality, there are a lot of considerations that go into getting the right vehicle for you.

Things to consider when purchasing a vehicle:

- Weather (Convertible, 4WD, Motorcycle)
- Distance (MPG or Miles per Charge)
- Number of Family Members
- Diesel/Gas/Hybrid/Electric
- Purpose (Truck, SUV, Sedan, Minivan)
- Security (Garage, Neighborhood)
- Cost (Total Monthly Cost):
  - Price
  - Insurance
  - Maintenance

Whether it is more financially advantageous to buy or lease a vehicle depends on various factors, including your financial situation, driving habits, and long-term plans. Here are some pros and cons of buying and leasing a vehicle to help you determine which option is best for you:

Pros of buying a vehicle:

- **Ownership:** When you buy a vehicle, you own it and can do with it as you please. This gives you more freedom and flexibility than leasing, as the lease agreement will limit which modifications you can make or the total mileage you can travel without being penalized.

- **Potential for no-payments:** If you can get a vehicle that lasts longer than the loan, you will have a period without payments. This is great as you are not used to having this money, so you can invest it, apply it to savings, or pay off another liability. However, there is a point where the maintenance and reliability of an older vehicle could outpace the cost of payments on a newer or more reliable car.
- **Lower long-term cost:** In the long run, buying a vehicle may be less expensive than leasing, especially if you get past payments. Also, you can sell/trade in the vehicle when you are ready to upgrade to a new one.

Cons of buying a vehicle:

- **Higher upfront cost:** Buying a vehicle typically requires a more significant upfront investment, as you must pay for the entire vehicle cost upfront or finance it with a loan.
- **Maintenance and repair costs:** As a vehicle owner, you are responsible for all maintenance and repair costs. These costs can add up over time and may be more expensive than your monthly payments if you leased a vehicle. **Pro Tip**: Don't buy an extended warranty from anyone who calls you on the phone.

Pros of leasing a vehicle:

- **Lower upfront cost:** Leasing a vehicle typically requires a lower upfront investment than buying, as you only have to pay for the portion of the vehicle's value that you use during the lease term. Unfortunately, the greatest depreciation is in the first few years.
- **Lower monthly payments:** Leasing a vehicle may also result in lower monthly payments than financing a vehicle purchase because, like above, you only pay for the portion of the vehicle's value you use during the lease term.
- **No need to sell the vehicle:** When you lease a vehicle, you do not have to worry about selling it when you are ready to upgrade to a new one. Instead, you return the leased vehicle and lease a new one.
- **Routine Maintenance:** Routine maintenance is often covered in the lease agreement.
- **Reliability:** You are getting a brand-new vehicle every term and can continue to swap out your vehicle indefinitely.
- **Military advantage:** If you are leasing a vehicle and receive deployment orders or orders to a location where personal vehicles are not authorized, you can turn in the vehicle with no penalties.

Cons of leasing a vehicle:

- **You have no equity in the vehicle:** You can't sell or use it for a trade-in unless you pay it off at the end of the term.
- **Can't personalize vehicle:** There are often restrictions to the amount of customization that can be done to the vehicle.

Whatever you decide (buy or lease), be sure to do your research on the vehicle. Some cars look great but have extensive maintenance issues. This often happens when it is a new type of vehicle or the manufacturer made a significant modification since the last model was sold (e.g., a new engine).

Financing

Get what you can easily afford. You should never allow a vehicle to take control of your finances. Keep in mind, no matter which vehicle you choose, you also have insurance, gas, and maintenance to pay for.

- **Overpayment/Extra Payment:** Regardless of what loan you get, pay above your minimum payment if you can. Like your mortgage, any additional money goes straight to the principal and will significantly reduce your loan period and overall interest paid. Make sure there is no prepayment penalty. The goal is to have a good car with no car payments for a few years. NOTE: In the last chapter, we discussed how making one extra payment yearly would save you time/money on your loan. The same is true for a vehicle loan. For example, if you financed $30,000 for five years at 6% interest, you pay about $580 a month. If you make an additional $580 payment each year (it doesn't have to be in one payment, it can be broken up over the year), you would cut 12 months off your loan, saving about $4,640.

- **Routine Maintenance:** Always do routine maintenance (oil, tires, brakes, etc.) If you can, learn to do it yourself. If you need more space/tools, see if your base/post has an Auto Hobby Shop. Those lights that came on near the speedometer aren't emojis.
- **New vs. Used Cars:** Buying a new car is almost always a money pit. Until recently, with supply chain issues and chip shortages, the value of a vehicle can drop as much as 50% as soon as it is driven off the car lot. Therefore, purchasing a used car is almost always more financially responsible. If a warranty is a concern, many used vehicles have warranties, or a reputable third-party warranty can always be purchased. Many times, if a car is used but has low mileage, the manufacturer's warranty can be transferred into the new purchaser's name. You have to

call the manufacturer, and they will send you the paperwork.

Money Pits

- **Sports/Luxury Cars:** I've seen many young Service Members buy sports cars. I get it, the money is rolling in, on paper you can afford it, and it looks awesome in the parking lot. What you need to understand are the ancillary expenses. Your insurance is going to be much higher, especially if you are under 25 or don't have a spotless driving record. Also, premium gas/diesel fuel and maintenance fees will be much higher. You must take all of these things into account when picking your vehicle. **Pro Tip**: If you just arrived at 4ID do not buy a rear-wheel drive sports car as your only vehicle. It snows in Colorado.
- **Repossession:** If you don't make the payments on your vehicle, it will be taken back, otherwise known as repossessed. This usually happens when you get in over your head. Even if you give the car back to the dealership, it counts as repossession and will hurt your credit rating.
- **Under/Not Insured:** The phrase "an accident waiting to happen" applies literally and figuratively here. Skimping on insurance is never a way to cut expenses.

- **Failure to Register:** I have seen a lot of expired plates recently. Many states have changed their laws stating police cannot initiate a traffic stop for expired tags. If you are pulled over for anything else, you will be charged and fined for expired plates. Also, not to call anyone out, but base cops won't hesitate to stop you and get you sideways with your leadership over expired tags. Just pay the fees.

3

Consumer Goods

"The one who can give the consumer the best quality at lower prices will certainly be the head of the industry, no matter what goods he produces. This is an immutable law."

~ Henry Ford

I know what you're thinking; here we go with a sermon on what not to buy. I'm sorry to disappoint you. As I've said, none of this is prescriptive. I only want to arm you with the best knowledge available, so you don't look back with regret, wishing you had or had not purchased a big-ticket item and find yourself in debt or broke at the end of your time in the military.

Let's be honest unless you are buying an asset (something that will make you money from its ownership), everything you purchase aside from food or services is a consumer good. This is considered discretionary spending, meaning a non-essential expense. These 'wants' rather than 'needs' greatly impact your ability or inability to accumulate long-term wealth.

Serving in the military can present some unique challenges when deciding for or against certain consumer goods; much of that has to do with value and durability. Like many of you, I judge items I consider buying with a few 'unique-to-military' concerns like, are the movers going to break this? When (not if) it gets damaged, can I get it repaired or replaced where I'm headed? Is this too nice, and there's a high probability that this gets 'lost' by the movers during my next PCS? Another question I ask myself is, how many times do I need to purchase this item? It's common to rebuy items that are a pain to move, such as lawnmowers, BBQs, and anything that runs on fuel. The same goes for items that may be predominately used in certain locations. I was the guy that took snowshoes and ice scrapers to Tampa, Florida, because I had already bought them twice before.

After ten moves in twenty-one years, I don't have a single set of matching silverware, I'm on my sixth or seventh ironing board, and I need a new snow shovel because I bought a super cheap one the last time. These are likely common to you all, and you could add an entire list based on your experiences. Maybe you have even purchased the same piece of IKEA furniture multiple times as I have. I'm not sure why the movers thought my TV stand could hold the weight of my washing machine.

This chapter will explore when it is better to buy higher quality items, when it is better to buy a more budget-friendly option, and when to pass on the purchase altogether. After taking a few of these recommendations, you will have saved some money perfect for investing in assets, as described in Chapter 15.

There are pros and cons to buying quality consumer goods over less expensive items that may have a higher failure rate. Here are some of the main points to consider:

Pros of buying quality consumer goods:

- **Higher durability:** Quality consumer goods are typically made with better materials and construction, which can make them more durable and less prone to breaking or malfunctioning. This can save you money in the long run, as you may have to replace the item less frequently.
- **Better performance:** Quality consumer goods are often designed to perform better than lower-quality alternatives. This can be particularly important for appliances, electronics, and tools you use frequently or rely on for important tasks.
- **Better warranty coverage:** Quality consumer goods often come with better warranty coverage, which can provide additional protection in the event that something goes wrong with the item.

Cons of buying quality consumer goods:

- **Higher upfront cost:** Quality consumer goods are generally more expensive than lower-quality alternatives, which can be a drawback for people who are looking to save money.
- **Limited availability:** Quality consumer goods may be available in fewer stores or online retailers than lower-quality alternatives, making it more difficult to find and purchase the items you want.
- **Less flexibility:** Quality consumer goods may offer fewer options or features than lower-quality alternatives.

While it's often true that you get what you pay for, there are times when buying a lower-quality consumer item may be the better option. Here are some scenarios in which it might be better to opt for a lower-quality item:

Pros of buying lower quality consumer goods:

- **Short-Term or Temporary Use:** If you only need the item for a short period of time or temporary use, it may be better to buy a lower-quality item. For example, if you're moving to a new apartment and need a cheap set of dishes to use until you can afford to upgrade, a lower-quality set may be a better option.

- **Infrequent Use:** If you only plan to use the item occasionally, investing in a high-quality, expensive option may prove wasteful. For example, a cheaper model may suffice if you only use a blender a few times a year.
- **Limited Budget:** A lower-quality item may be the best option if you have a limited budget and need more money to afford to invest in a high-quality item. For example, a lower-quality laptop may still meet your needs if you need a new laptop for work or school but need more money to afford a high-end model.
- **Disposable Items:** Some items are meant to be disposable, and investing in a high-quality option may not make sense. For example, if you're hosting a party and need disposable plates and utensils, it may be more cost-effective to buy a lower-quality, disposable option.
- **Experimentation:** If you're trying something new and are curious if you'll like it or use it frequently, buying a lower-quality item to test it out may be better. For example, if you're interested in taking up a new hobby like painting or photography, consider starting with a lower-quality, entry-level item to see if you enjoy it before investing in more expensive equipment.

While buying lower-quality consumer goods may seem like a cost-effective option in the short term, there are several potential downfalls to consider:

Cons of buying low-quality consumer goods:

- **Durability:** Lower-quality consumer goods are often less durable than their more expensive counterparts. They may break, wear out, or stop working sooner, leading to more frequent replacements and ultimately costing more in the long term.
- **Performance:** Lower-quality goods may not perform as well as more expensive alternatives, which can be frustrating and ultimately lead to the need for replacement. For example, a cheaper kitchen knife may not cut as well, leading to a more frustrating and time-consuming cooking experience.
- **Safety:** Lower-quality goods may not meet safety standards, which can be hazardous to users. For example, cheaper electrical products may not have adequate safety features and can pose a risk of fire or electric shock.
- **Environmental Impact:** Lower-quality goods may not be environmentally friendly, as they are often made from lower-quality materials that are not sustainably sourced or produced. Additionally, the need for more frequent replacements of lower-quality goods can contribute to increased waste.
- **Reputation:** Buying low-quality goods can damage your reputation and credibility. For example, if a professional photographer showed up to your wedding and only

brought a disposable camera, you would rightfully be concerned with their credibility.

Overall, the pros and cons of buying quality consumer goods over less expensive items that may have a higher failure rate depend on your individual circumstances and priorities.

Pro Tip: Learn to fix items yourself versus replacing them. There are videos on YouTube on how to diagnose and fix almost anything. Amazon can get you replacement parts the next day. In many cases, you can fix an issue even before you can get a repair person to your house, and you don't have to pay just for them to show up.

With the advent of 3D printing, the cost of replacement parts is falling. But, unfortunately, the price of service (i.e., house calls) is not.

Before you buy, compare products online (e.g., Consumer Reports, YouTube, product reviews). Make a comparison with one or more comparable products. Then you can avoid an underpowered, overpriced, breakdown-prone item.

Money Pits

- Avoid products with lots of moving parts or 'advanced' electronics. Do you need a refrigerator with a touch screen you can play chess on? It doesn't make the food colder. More is not always better. Sometimes more is just more things to break.
- Not doing your research and buying products with known and reported defects.

4

Pets

"Animals are such agreeable friends- they ask no questions; they pass no criticisms."

~ George Eliot

As I type the introduction to this chapter, my two-year-old golden retriever named Theodore, call sign "Teddy," sleeps under my desk. As dumb as he looks with his tongue sticking to the floor, he is the one creature on the planet I would fight a bear to defend.

Teddy is the first dog I have ever owned as an adult, and that was by design. For me, it was strictly logistics. I knew I wanted to get some overseas assignments, and I didn't know, nor care to learn, how to navigate those hurdles with a pet. It was difficult enough trying to do it correctly as an adult. Although I didn't know it then, my decision made a lot of financial sense too. In this chapter, we are going to talk about all the expenses tied to pet ownership. I know pet owners like me are going to hate this chapter, but this is a finance book, and the facts don't lie. Having a pet is nearly as expensive as having a child. In some cases, it could be much more, depending on if there are some health issues that you are forced to pay for out of pocket.

While it is true that the financial burden varies based on the type of pet you have, whether dog, cat, chinchilla, horse, rabbit, pot-bellied pig, chicken, bearded dragon, or ferret, all will cost you money that you could otherwise be investing. If you are set on a family tarantula, so be it. I'll make some recommendations for you to take care of Fluffy on a budget and be prepared for unforeseen health issues.

Pets are great emotional support and can also provide a sense of security. They are always happy to see you after a long day at work. Keep in mind pets are living creatures and have needs of their own.

The cost of a family pet over its life can vary widely depending on the type of pet, its size, its breed, as well as your location, and the level of care you provide. However, here are some general estimates of the costs of owning a pet over its lifetime:

- **Cats:** The average cost of owning a cat over its lifetime is around $17,000, according to the American Society for the Prevention of Cruelty to Animals (ASPCA).[xii]

This estimate includes costs such as food, litter, veterinary care, and other supplies.

- **Dogs:** The average cost of owning a dog over its lifetime is around $22,000, according to the ASPCA.[xiii] This estimate includes expenses such as food, training, veterinary care, and other supplies. The cost of owning a dog can vary widely depending on the size and breed of the dog, with larger breeds generally costing more to own. NOTE: Those new to dog ownership may need to learn this. You have to keep up with your pet's dental care as well as physical health. Tartar buildup and rotting teeth can cause problems for your pet's overall health. Also, it is not cheap because they have to put your dog under anesthesia to do dental work.

"Hi! Do you have any snacks?"

~ Theodore "Teddy" Nolan

- **Small animals:** The cost of owning a small animal, such as a hamster, guinea pig, rabbit, reptile, or fish, is generally lower than the cost of owning a cat or dog. However, these pets still require food, bedding, cages, tanks, and other supplies, which can add up over time.

It's important to remember that these estimates are just rough averages and do not consider your pet's specific needs or circumstances. For example, a pet with health issues or special needs may require additional veterinary care or other expenses, which could increase the overall cost of ownership.

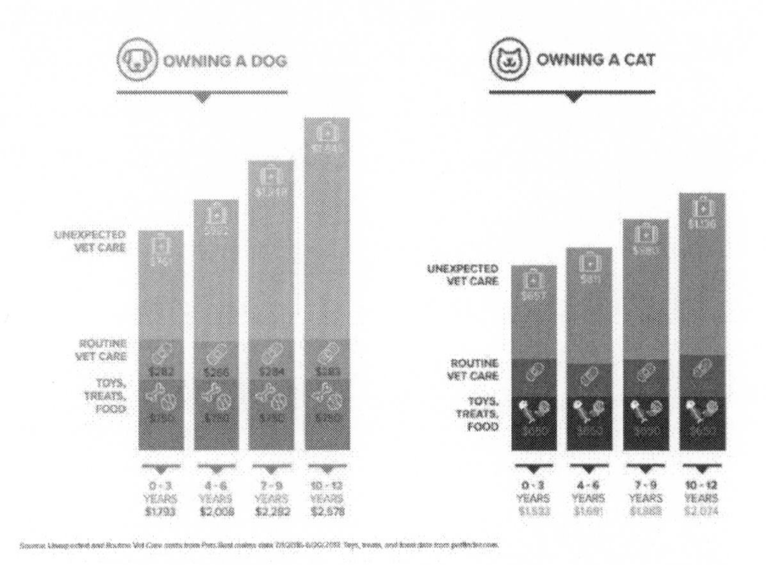

Other Costs/Issues:

- **Pet Deposits/Fees:** Most apartments require additional fees for pets. You may be able to get this waived if your pet is classified as a therapy or service animal.
- **Allergies:** This may seem like common sense, but make sure you do not have animal allergies before bringing it home.

- **Do your Research:** Some pets have specific needs or have chronic health issues. For example, a larger dog may require a large yard or frequent walks. Some are better around crowds or children. Some are just haters (damn you, chihuahuas). There are also limitations on moving pets between states to avoid invasive species. This is more geared toward exotic pets like some reptiles and ferrets.
- **Pet Boarding:** If you travel or deploy frequently, you will have to find someone or somewhere to take care of your pets. This is often expensive (upwards of $100/day) unless you have a friend willing to help out.
- **Pet Insurance:** You and your family have health insurance. What about your pets? They get sick and hurt as well. Veterinary services are costly, especially if you have to go in after hours or on the weekend. I recommend pet insurance but don't pay more than $50/month.[xiv] This could be the one decision that prevents you from a massive, unexpected bill.
- Overall, owning a pet can be a rewarding experience, but it is also a significant financial responsibility. Therefore, it's a good idea to carefully consider the costs of owning a pet and make sure you are prepared to meet the financial obligations of pet ownership before bringing a pet into your home.
- **Multiple Pets:** Having more than one pet can significantly inhibit housing options as many property

managers have strict limits not only on breed/size but also limit the number of pets to one.

Money Pits

- **Puppy Mills:** Get your pets from reputable breeders. Puppy mills churn out dogs so fast they are likely to have health or genetic issues. Getting a dog from a professional breeder will also minimize the predisposition of bad health often realized by owners of rescue animals.

5

Insurance

"No matter how much you are earning or how much you have saved, your financial position can be dented by an unexpected event in a moment."

~ Iffco Toiko

One day an insurance salesman was approached by a crook. The crook stopped the salesman and said, "I don't like what you are up to. Stop giving guys like me a bad name."

If it's one thing I hate, it's paying for insurance. Month after month, year after year, rates go up, and I have nothing to show for it. As an unmarried male in my 40s, it still costs me hundreds of dollars monthly for insurance I hope never to use.

As military members, there are specific perks available to you that will be discussed in this chapter. Many of them may also apply to former military and their families. Ultimately, if you drive, you will have to pay for auto insurance. In addition, you will need life insurance if you are married or have someone in your family who relies on you financially. I will recommend a few other types of insurance in this chapter, like home or renters' policies and pet insurance. Each of them feels like you are throwing your money out the window, but each will ultimately prevent you from derailing your savings and investment plan.

Disasters happen all the time. This chapter aims to ensure that one car wreck, break-in, or case of feline leukemia doesn't break your bank balance and jeopardize your financial freedom. A few years ago, a fence blew down at my house during a storm. I had just returned from leave, where I had spent way too much of my savings on transportation, hotels, and food. I was not in a position to repair or replace the fence, especially after I received an estimate of more than five thousand dollars. This was the one time I was happy that I had a homeowner's policy that covered the repairs. I put the five-hundred-dollar deductible on a credit card and devised a plan to pay it off in my budget. This was a case where, had I not been insured, a sum of just five thousand dollars could have set me back for years.

I still think all insurance companies are bloodsuckers. Still, after all these years of paying much more in insurance than I have ever received, I believe it is the appropriate recommendation for you all. Consider this a defensive tactic against an unknown enemy.

Life Insurance:

Here's a scary thought, your military retirement pay stops when you die. If you are the primary earner in your family, your absence could mean ruin for your family. Life insurance aims to replace your income when you pass to take care of your obligations and your family. Think about your family losing you and their financial security at the same time. Okay, Debbie Downer moment complete.

- **Serviceman's Group Life Insurance (SGLI):**[xv] SGLI is an easy button, and there is no reason to opt-out. Besides that, it's pretty cheap for what you get. At this time, it's currently six cents per one thousand dollars of coverage up to $500K ($30/month).
  This is a great benefit, don't pass it up. For more information on SGLI, go to the following website: https://www.va.gov/life-insurance/options-eligibility/sgli/.
- **Veteran's Group Life Insurance (VGLI):**[xvi] When you retire, you can swap from SGLI to VGLI within one year and 120 days from discharge. However, you can only get up to the amount you were getting under SGLI and the monthly rates depend upon your age. It's simple to join and rates remain consistently lower than commercial competitors. For more information on VGLI, go to the

following website: https://www.va.gov/life-insurance/options-eligibility/vgli/.

Non-military Insurance:[xvii]

- **Whole Life:** Provides insurance for your entire life and comes with a cash value component that grows over time. There are some creative programs like infinite banking, where your life insurance policy can become a constant access to cash. The problem is it ties your insurance with investing. So, if you do buy a Whole Life plan, make sure to do your research and read the fine print. In my opinion, you can make higher returns through different investment vehicles.
- **Term Life:** Provides insurance for a set period of time (usually between ten - thirty years). The rate will remain constant for the term of the policy. I recommend a Term Life policy as the most cost-effective option.

Other Insurance:

- **Renter's Insurance:** Even if you don't own your home, you should insure everything inside it.
- **Specialty Insurance:** Certain areas require additional insurance for high-risk factors like fire and flood.

- **Umbrella Insurance:**[xviii] Umbrella insurance is extra insurance that provides protection beyond the existing limits and coverage of other policies. It allows you to select your liability limit and best protect your assets. If you have rental properties, I recommend an umbrella policy.
- **Additional Insurance:** If you use your home or auto in a non-traditional manner (e.g., rental property or Uber/Lyft, respectively), you may require additional insurance.
- **Pet Insurance:** As discussed in the last chapter, pets getting sick or hurt can cause serious financial burdens.
- **Health Insurance:** While you are in the military, you typically do not have to worry about health insurance for yourself or your spouse. For those of you who cohabitate with a significant other that is not your legal spouse, it is critical you understand how medical issues for them will be paid for and, if necessary, secure medical insurance. Not having health insurance is the leading cause of bankruptcies (66.5%) in America due to the high cost of care as well as time out of work.[xix]

Once you separate from the military, medical, dental, and vision care can be purchased on the open market. Make sure you have a plan before your last day in uniform. If you retire from the military, Tricare has proven (for me personally) to be a good provider at a reasonable price.

Money Pits

- YOLO: You only live once, but you don't want to be paying off medical debt stemming from an unexpected accident for the rest of your life.
- Youth≠Invincibility: Trust me, you can get hurt. The medical system doesn't care if you are young, you will be saddled with huge expenses. Get insurance and take precautions. The risk is not worth the reward.

6

Deployments, TDYs, and Travel

"Jobs fill your pockets, but adventure fills your soul."

~ Dana Berez

If you are anything like me, one of your motivations for joining the military was the chance to go and see the world and be paid to do it. When I found out what my job was going to be, I was pretty disappointed to find out that the training base was only four hours from where I lived. So much for seeing the world. The dreams in my head of eating sushi in Japan and Italian food prepared by *real* Italians were dashed. If you can't tell, I love food, and most of my dreams include the perceived luxury of living abroad and eating their local cuisine. Although it would take me another year, I am happy to report that the military allowed me to live in many foreign countries. Some were absolutely amazing, and others amazingly dusty and filled with people who wanted to kill me. Each of them had a lot of food I enjoyed and, more importantly, allowed me to learn about their cultures, languages, histories, and peoples.

Aside from summer car trips, I did not travel much as a kid. My perception was that any and all travel was expensive, especially overseas travel. However, the military taught me that the world is an amazingly large place and there is so much to explore. Navigating foreign places isn't terribly difficult when you have access to Wi-Fi and Google Translate. During my first overseas assignment, I am sad to report, I used my mid-tour leave to come home rather than go exploring. As I got older, in my 20s-30s, I built up the courage to join acquaintances or solo travel in countries surrounding my overseas duty stations.

Although I don't sport a compass tattoo or 1K flight status on any major airline, I learned the right and wrong way to budget for travel. It can be challenging to say no to buying everyone you know a souvenir from a far-off place. Likewise, it can be equally difficult not to buy the cliché lederhosen in Germany, wool sweater in Iceland, kimono in Japan, or kilt in Scotland. I'm here to tell you I've bought many of them and moved from assignment to assignment with them. Yet I rarely, if ever, wore them after I departed that country.

There are so many fantastic travel benefits to being in the military. This chapter will break them down and allow you and your family (if applicable) to create lasting memories. I will also provide some lesser-known travel hacks specific to the military, like how to not burn all your leave while waiting on Space-A travel, how to pay half price for a getaway by bringing your travel partner with you TDY/TAD, or how to add leave to your orders to maximize city-pair air travel. This may be your favorite chapter if you are looking for life hacks. So please place your tray tables in the upright and locked position, and let's get ready for takeoff.

Deployments:

Military deployment can be a stressful and uncertain time for the Service Member and their family. Here are a few financial considerations to keep in mind before deploying:

- **Make a budget:** Determine how much money you will need to cover your expenses while you are deployed, and make a budget to ensure that your bills will be paid. If possible, try to save some extra money in case of emergencies that could pop up while you are gone.
- **Update your will:** If you need to do so, create/update your will before deploying. This will ensure that your wishes are carried out in the event of your death.
- **Powers of Attorney (POA):**[xx] Set up a POA as needed. A POA gives someone the legal authority to make decisions on your behalf. As such, make sure you give

them only to someone you trust and who knows your interests and intentions. They are usually used when you are not available to sign legal documents. A durable power of attorney will work if you are ill or disabled. Be sure to understand the different types and uses of POAs. You don't want to inadvertently give away everything you own by mistake. The different types of POAs are:

- Health Care Power of Attorney (HCPOA)
- Financial Power of Attorney
- General Power POA
- Limited POA
- Durable Power of Attorney (DPOA)

- **Update your insurance:** Make sure your insurance coverage is current and sufficient to protect your family in your absence. This can include life insurance, health insurance, and homeowners' or renters' insurance. Also, make sure your beneficiaries are up to date.
- **Make a plan for your debts:** If you have debts, make a plan for how they will be paid while you are deployed. If necessary, you may be able to postpone or reduce your payments temporarily. Sometimes, you only need to provide a copy of your orders.
- **Coordinate with your spouse or family:** If you have a spouse or family, make sure they know what to do in case

of an emergency and how to access your financial accounts. It may be helpful to provide them with copies of important documents, such as your will, insurance policies, and power of attorney.

- **Other liabilities:** Put club memberships on hold. If you are going overseas for more than 90 days, you can put your Officers/NCO/Enlisted club membership on hold. Some other ideas include:

    - Set up Autopay for bills or, at least, electronic billing so you can do it from wherever you are.
    - Call your insurance company to tell them that you are traveling and to place your vehicle in 'storage' status.
    - Call your cell phone company to either put your account on hold or add overseas roaming while you're gone.
    - If you are renting, let your landlord know you will be gone.
    - Have someone regularly check on your residence while you are gone and check your mail for any unexpected bills or checks.

- **Specialty pay:** Understand and ensure you receive any specialty pay for the region you are going to, such as:

- Career Sea Pay
- Diving Duty Pay
- Hardship Duty Pay
- Hazardous Duty Incentive Pay
- Hostile Fire/Imminent Danger Pay
- Overseas Extension Pay
- Special Warfare Pay
- Submarine Pay
- Family Separation
- Combat Zone Tax Exclusion
- TSP tax-free contribution

TDY/TAD:

When you travel, you are given a daily food allowance. Unlike your lodging expenses, if you don't spend it, you get to keep it. Trust me; it is possible to spend less on food than they give you. You don't have to go crazy, like taking a suitcase of ramen and Pop-Tarts with you. I know someone who did, and they ended up in the emergency room (that's a story for another time).

If you are staying off base/post, ensure you get a non-availability letter from lodging. Without it, they are only obligated to refund you the base/post rate. Make sure whatever hotel you get is under the government rate limit. If you can't find one, you can ask in advance for a waiver and be paid the actual cost. You should never be required to pay out of pocket for expenses associated with official travel if you have done the proper coordination.

- **Sightseeing:** Use your nights and weekends to get out and see the sights. Far too often, those on travel spend their nights in their rooms or out drinking. You never know when you might return. I recommend taking advantage of the free trip.

Bring your significant other or a friend/family member to visit when you are on official travel. If you are lucky enough to be sent somewhere that folks can visit you, look into bringing them for part of the time. In addition to spending time together, it will allow them to see where you go and what you do when you leave. It also saves you the lodging expense since most hotel rooms come with two beds. For example, I saved thousands by having friends meet me in Las Vegas, Hawaii, or elsewhere. I was being paid to be there, and after work each day, I got to share a fun trip with my travel partners.

- **City pair:** This technique can be a little complicated, but it can also unlock a bunch of travel options for you. Put simply, the government has a set rate it will pay up to for the cost of a round trip, reimbursable airline ticket. This is called the city pair. As long as you remain within the rule set of the Joint Travel Regulation and don't do anything illegal, you could carve out a little slice of time for yourself. For example, if I was required to go to a one-week conference in a city half-way across the country and the city pair price for the round trip airfare is $1500, I could opt to make it a road trip as long as my expenses didn't exceed the city pair price. This travel time has to be approved but I know plenty of folks that do this to get some 'free leave'. What you are doing, in effect, is saving the government money on airfare and perhaps rental car expenses at the duty location. Anytime travel is involved and you can save the government money, the chances are high you will be approved and maybe even commended for being a good steward of tax payer money.

Leave:

When you take time off to travel, there are ways that your military service can save you money.

- **Leave in Conjunction with orders:** If you are lucky enough to go TDY/TAD, you can take leave while you are there. This will save you the round-trip ticket. Of course, you may have to check out of the hotel and turn in the rental car in order to keep the receipts separate, but this is far less expensive than taking the trip with your own money.

- **Space Available (Space-A) Travel:** If a military aircraft is flying somewhere and there is excess seating, it is possible to fly for free or for the cost of a box lunch. It is all done on a Space-A basis. You have to be on leave to sign up, but there is a trick (at least for the Air Force, all others should check your service-specific leave policies/applications to verify). Enter your leave in Leave Web to get a leave number. Now you can sign up for Space-A travel. If you don't make it on the flight, log in, cancel your leave, and go to work. If you make the flight, your leave is in the system. One caution to Space-A is that just because you catch a flight out does not mean you will be able to get Space-A for your return. Always make sure you have enough money to buy a ticket back, if necessary.
- **Government Rates:** When you book your hotel, ask if they have a government rate. These are usually lower, but not always. You usually only have to show your Military ID card when you check-in. This goes the same for plane flights and rental cars. It never hurts to ask. Don't stop there, ask for AAA, Senior Citizen, AARP, etc. discounts, as applicable. If you can help it, never pay full price.
- **Billeting:** If hotels are too expensive where you want to go, see if there is a nearby base/post. There is usually limited availability that is aimed at TDY personnel, but if

you can get in, your rate will be cheaper than downtown and the cost is usually subsidized for junior ranks.

- **Armed Forces Recreation Centers:**[xxi] **(Shades of Green / Hali Koa / Dragon Hill / Edelweiss)** The military has some amazing recreation resorts around the globe, spanning Hawaii, Florida, South Korea, and Germany. Be sure to sign up well in advance and your rate will be based on your rank. Additionally there are vendors such as Armed Forces Vacation Club (https://www.afvclub.com/) that cater to military and veterans looking to travel on a budget. Utilizing these benefits will save you hundreds to thousands on every trip.
- **Rental cars:** Sometimes the weekly rate is less than the daily rate multiplied by how long you are going to be there. Ask if there is an issue with you returning the car early.
- **USO:** Most major airports have a USO lounges (United Service Organizations). It is a quiet, safe place to hang out if you have a layover. They also tend to have free snacks and drinks for active duty members and their families.
- **Rideshare (e.g., Uber & Lyft) vs Rental Car:** If you are not going to be using a vehicle continuously when you are on leave, it might make more sense to use a rideshare platform when you need a lift. This will also save you parking fees at your hotel.

- **Short-Term Home Rental (Airbnb, VACASA, VRBO) vs. Hotel:** If you are traveling with a group, it may be cheaper to rent out a house for everyone vs. getting multiple rooms in a hotel.

Money Pits

- Screwing up the exchange rates and spending too much money on an overseas TDY or vacation.
- Using your government travel card (GTC) for anything except official government travel. This could result in Non-Judicial Punishment (NJP). Don't take out your cash advance from an ATM at a casino or other unspeakable location.
- Not saving receipts over $75.
- Returning from official travel without a non-availability letter when you stayed off base/post.
- Not setting up overseas roaming on your cell phone in advance...very costly.
- Time Shares. Don't do it, not ever. Really, don't.

7

Taxes

"The hardest thing in the world to understand is income tax."

~ Albert Einstein

If nothing is certain but death and taxes, then I say cheat both. In this case, I am not recommending anyone do anything illegal, but rather the opposite. I want each of you to do everything legally acceptable to have a long life and pay only the absolute legal minimum in taxes. Taxes are the single largest expense you will have in your entire life. By becoming an informed taxpayer and understanding how the very wealthy legally avoid paying a ton in taxes, you will have more in your pocket to accumulate and save.

Taxes come in all sorts of shapes and forms; this chapter will be primarily educational. We will examine the most common tax types that impact you and how you can keep more of your money for yourself and your family. We will cover federal and state income tax, property tax, sales tax, and capital gains tax. By breaking down each one and giving you some military-specific insights, you will increase your overall take and be on your way to financial freedom.

Disclaimer, I am not a certified tax planner, but I will tell you to be wary of anyone who says they are. When dealing with federal income tax, I recommend against you going it alone and submitting through Turbo Tax. Personally, I have tried them all, bookkeepers, tax preparers, CPAs, and doing my own. Sadly, many tax professionals follow a simple adherence strategy versus a customized plan for you specifically. They want the simplest returns in and out so they can make their money and move on. Military members have special dispensation when it comes to tax law, learning about these exemptions and taking advantage of them may be the best advice in this entire book. Too many military members overpay taxes. Let's go get you your money.

There are several ways that a person can consistently minimize their tax obligations:

- **Contribute to a retirement account:** Contributions to certain types of retirement accounts, such as a 401(k) or traditional IRA, may be tax-deductible. This is the simplest way to reduce your taxable income and lower your tax bill.

  - Thrift Savings Plan (Automatic, 3%)[xxii]
  - 401K
  - Individual Retirement Accounts (IRAs)
    - Traditional IRA
    - Roth IRA
  - Saver's Credit[xxiii]

- **Consider your filing status:** Your tax rate and the amount of taxes you owe may depend on your filing status. For example, married couples may be able to save on taxes by filing a joint return rather than separate returns.
- **Take advantage of tax credits and deductions:** There are a number of tax credits and deductions available that can reduce your tax bill. For example, you may be able to claim a credit for education expenses or a deduction for charitable donations or child care costs.
- **Keep good records:** It's essential to keep good records of your income and expenses, as this can help you to claim all the credits and deductions you are entitled to. It is very difficult to prove your past. Unfortunately credit card statements do not count as receipts.
- **Use tax software or a tax professional:** Tax software and tax professionals can help you minimize your tax obligations by ensuring that you take advantage of all the credits and deductions you are eligible for. However, I

don't trust my ability to input everything correctly into the tax software. I also don't trust a random individual that may not understand specific rules for Service Members. I do recommend the volunteers that come on post/base every year around tax time. They will be an excellent resource for you.

- **Stay informed:** Tax laws can change from year to year, so it's important to stay knowledgeable about any changes that may affect you. This can help you to minimize your tax obligations and make sure you are paying the correct amount of taxes. Sites like Nerdwallet are a great place to stay informed about changes.
- **Consider your tax bracket:** Your tax bracket determines the rate at which your income is taxed. By understanding your tax bracket and how it is calculated, you can structure your income and deductions in a way that minimizes your tax bill. Your scheduled pay raises could actually place you in a bracket where you make less money. Be sure to stay ahead of this trap by adjusting your investment contributions when you get promoted or a scheduled raise.
- **Set your deductions appropriately:** Ideally, you should break even when you file your taxes. If you get a refund, it means you overpaid all year and the government has been earning interest on your money, not you. Hopefully there will never come a time when you

owe money, as it will possibly come as a surprise. This is most likely to happen if you sell a rental property or sell stocks and make a profit. If this occurs and you are in a bind, you can set up a payment plan with the IRS, so you don't have to pay it all at once.

- **If you owe money:** Adjust your deductions to make sure it doesn't happen again. In the meantime, you can request an income tax filing extension or set up a payment plan. Never choose to cash in your investments to pay a tax bill. This will actually hurt you twice. You will derail your future wealth and be taxed on the money you cash out. Depending on what you liquidate, you may also be forced to pay an additional 10% penalty.
- **Property tax**: As explained in Chapter 1, property taxes, usually paid twice a year, can force you to have a large sum of money ready to pay every six months. To avoid this, be sure to pay into an escrow account as part of your mortgage payment.
- **Sales tax:** Shop on base. There is no sales tax at the BX/PX/NEX. These savings could be substantial on high-ticket items like appliances which they sell on base.
- **Capital Gains Tax:**[xxiv] When selling assets, capital gains tax is collected on the money made by the seller. This tax rate can vary depending on how long you held the asset. Normally you must hold the asset for one year to minimize your exposure to this tax. The reason I'm not

too fond of day trading is because of the obscenely high short-term capital gains tax rate associated with the gains.

- **Deployment Tax-Free zones:** If you deploy to a combat zone, your military pay should be fully or partially tax free. This goes for bonuses received in country as well as TSP contributions.
- **State income tax:** The tax taken out of your military pay is based on the state of legal residence you claim. You do not have to change it every time you move. If you get stationed in a state with low- or no-income tax, you should highly consider changing your residency. Be aware some states, like Alaska, have requirements to maintain your residency. There are some states where you don't pay state income tax as a resident as long as you are stationed outside your home state, like California.[xxv] The Military Spouses Residency Relief Act allows military spouses to declare the same state of legal residency as their spouse. The Veterans Benefits and Transition Act allows spouses to make that choice regardless of when they were married. Selecting a favorable state to minimize taxes can be complicated depending on a number of factors, like where you have lived, when you entered active duty, and where you are currently stationed. If you are currently paying state income tax on your active duty pay, I recommend you contact your base legal office and/or finance office to determine your options. A couple of

quick conversations could save you thousands in the long run.

- **State Tax Breaks Available for Military and Retirees:** Take a look at http://wwww.military.com/money/personal-finance/ state-tax-information.html for more information.

Money Pits

- Not paying your taxes or not reporting all your income. The IRS may find out and come after you for the correct amount owed, plus interest.
- Paying more taxes than are owed out of convenience or due to lack of understanding.
- Not knowing your federal income tax rate and being forced to pay taxes at the end of the year because you needed to adjust the withholdings.
- Receiving a large tax refund that you could have otherwise invested for your future.
- Blowing your tax refund on stuff you don't need.

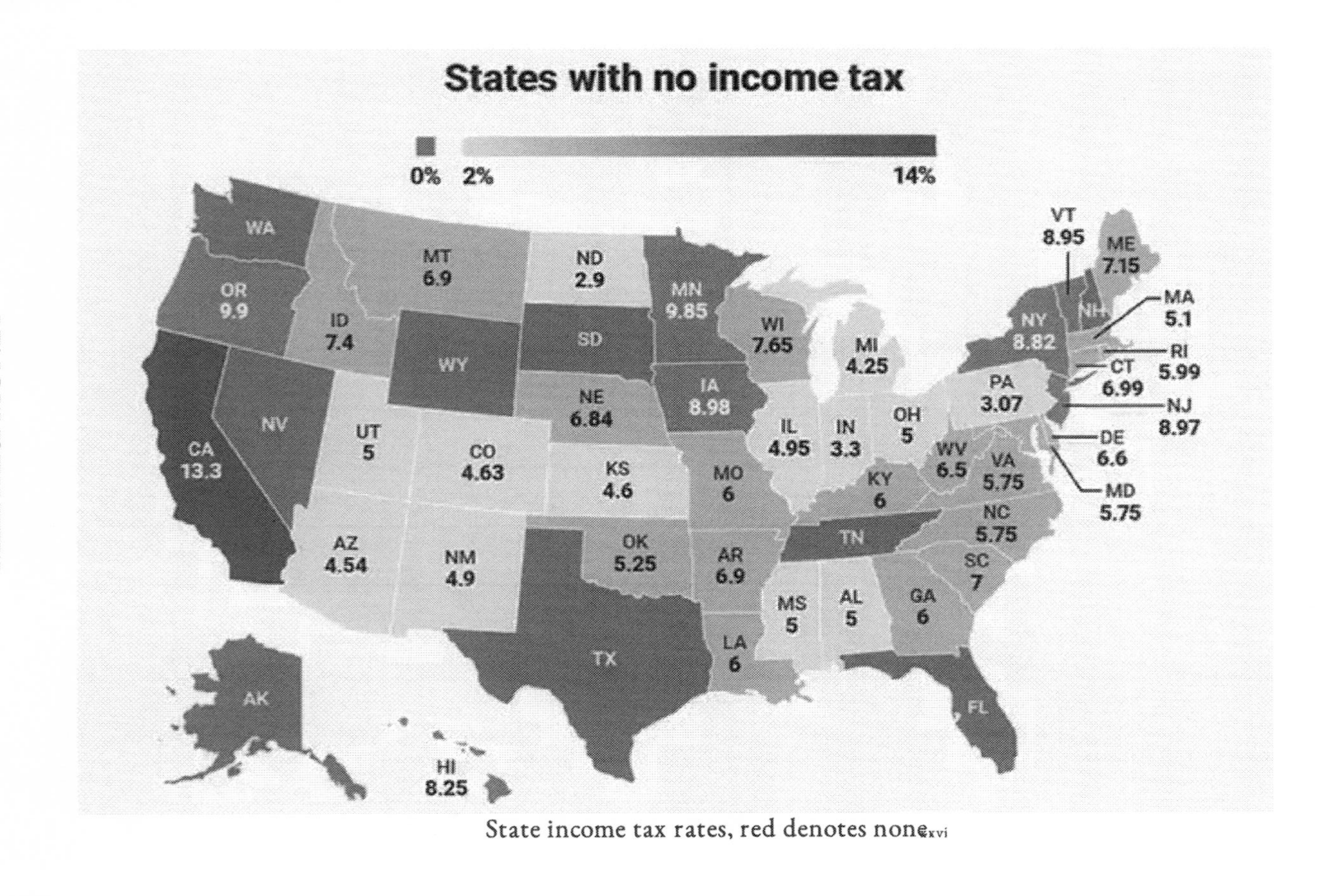

State income tax rates, red denotes none[xvi]

8

Education

"An investment in education always pays the highest returns."

~ Benjamin Franklin

The single best investment you can make is an investment in yourself. For many, that means education. But don't automatically think education always equals school. Although it can mean traditional schooling, education can take many forms. Luckily, the DoD understands that and has programs that make it easier than ever to get an education.

You may be asking, 'Why is education a chapter in this book about money?' The answer is simple. When you move on from the military, and that day comes for us all, the educated will make way more money than those who are not. I'm not talking a few extra dollars an hour; I mean hundreds of thousands to millions of dollars more over your remaining employed lives. Does that mean I want everyone who reads this to all go out and become doctors and lawyers? No. I am saying that those with a plan that they execute while on active duty have an opportunity to outpace their civilian peers, accumulate very little to no debt, and position themselves for a high-paying job upon separation. If you utilize even one or two of the educational opportunities available to you while serving in the military, you will have access to lifelong income. If that sounds interesting to you, I encourage you to keep reading.

This chapter will discuss the basics of tuition assistance, the GI Bill, and the different services COOL (Credentialing Opportunities On-Line) programs. We will also discuss free online classes, professional certifications, and trade schools. Each of these roads will lead you to an abundance of money and you need only choose the path that will get you to your intended target.

Are there exceptions to these opportunities? Absolutely. If you take the time to envision your ideal future life, understand what education is required to get there, and start knocking out those educational requirements now, you will be on your way to long-term high earnings. The best time to start is today and the worst time is tomorrow. This chapter is about action; educate yourself with purpose today.

There are three types of education to focus on in the military. First, your Professional Military Education (PME) includes your leadership schools. Your formal academic education includes Associates, Bachelors, Master, and Doctorate programs. Some in-resident Leadership PME can also earn you formal academic credit. Finally, there are alternative education methods like certifications and specialized trade schools. These are the types I routinely see people seek out at the end of their military service so they will be prepared for a post-military career.

PME: Beyond military history and leadership, PME will give you great experience with speaking, briefing and writing. These skills will all translate to any job you have after the military. PME is free and often required for promotion or advancement. The one thing to be aware of prior to attending any PME course is the Active-Duty Service Commitment (ADSC) that comes with in-residence training. If you are considering separating or retiring, be sure you understand the payback requirements before attending. In residence PME may award you an AA, BA, or MA degree. Deployments can be a great place/time to work on distance learning education. In addition, some overseas locations may host a testing center where you can continue to advance academically while you are away from home.

Formal Academic Education: Never rely on your service's promise to mask your formal education at selective boards. In my career, I saw it swing in both directions. Always complete the formal education requirements expected for your grade. In the military, the faster and more often you get promoted, the more money you make during your service. Continuing your formal academic education will make you competitive over your peers and provide you fodder for your future civilian resume.

Quick tips: Almost all bases/posts (and often in deployed locations) have an education center to assist you.

- When starting a program, make sure you can continue your education at your next duty station, either at the same school or that you can transfer completed credits. If not, you risk completing more credit hours than required.
- Get an associate degree as soon as you can. It will put you ahead of your peers with just a high-school education. This will fast-track you to promotion and higher pay.
- Get a bachelor's degree as soon as practical.
- Only attend accredited schools. There are a lot of institutions that prey upon the military because of your GI Bill or tuition assistance. So, make sure your school is accredited and preferably a not-for-profit institution.

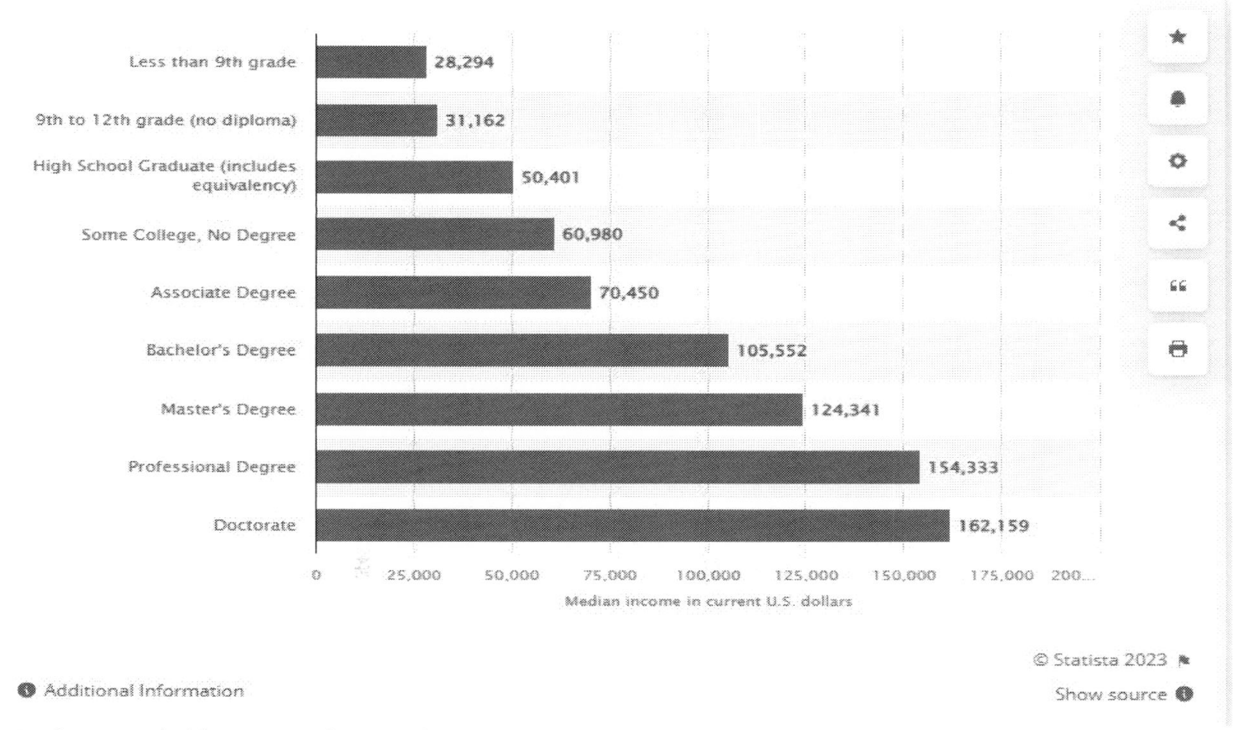

Median Household Income in the United States in 2021, by educational attainment of householder (In US Dollars) xxvii

Scholarships: Look around for scholarships. Ask the education office for advice and search the web. Many scholarships go unclaimed every year.

- Google search for unique scholarships. For example, many local banks will have scholarships, you have to ask for details or find them on their websites.

Grants: Grants are given based on financial need. The Department of Education offers three types of grants.[xxviii]

- **Discretionary grants:** awarded using a competitive process.
- **Student loans or grants:** to help students attend college.
- **Formula grants:** uses formulas determined by Congress and has no application process.

Tuition Assistance (TA):[xxix] The US military will pay for you to attend school. This amount varies and there is usually a cap on total assistance. Often TA will also provide money for books. The only requirement is you must pass every course. If not, you have to pay the money back. There is also an ADSC associated with TA so keep this in mind when you are considering a separation date.

College-Level Examination Program (CLEP):[xxx] There are also tests that will allow you to gain college credit by examination for certain classes through DANTES by demonstrating proficiency in the material by proctored test. This is a great benefit and is offered completely free.

Language Training: At some duty locations, free language training is offered. I saw this first in Qatar and then at a very low cost of $35 in Germany. Being bilingual, especially in Spanish in the US, can open many doors for jobs and volunteer positions. As an added bonus, some language proficiency may put more money in your paycheck (5-20% per hour).[xxxi]

The GI Bill[xxxii]

The GI Bill, also known as the Servicemen's Readjustment Act of 1944, is a program that provides education and training benefits to Veterans of the U.S. military. The GI Bill covers a wide range of education and training programs, including college or university degree programs, vocational or technical training, apprenticeships, and on-the-job training. The GI Bill also covers the cost of tuition and fees, as well as a monthly housing allowance and a stipend for books and supplies.

The GI Bill is administered by the U.S. Department of Veterans Affairs (VA) and is available to Veterans who have served on active duty and meet certain eligibility requirements. The GI Bill has undergone several changes since it was first enacted in 1944, and there are now several different versions of the program, including the Post-9/11 GI Bill, which was implemented in 2009.

The GI Bill is a significant benefit for Veterans, as it can help them to pursue higher education and training and build new careers after leaving the military. The GI Bill has helped millions of Veterans to further their education and transition to civilian life and it continues to be an important resource for current and former members of the military.

There are several benefits and potential drawbacks to transferring your GI Bill to your children:

Benefits:

- You can use the GI Bill to defray the education costs for one or more of your children.
- The housing stipend can be used for room and board.

Drawbacks:

- You will no longer be able to use the GI Bill for yourself.
- You may not be able to transfer the GI Bill back to yourself: Once you transfer the GI Bill to your children,

you may not be able to transfer it back to yourself, even if your children do not use all of the benefits.

- Your children may not be eligible to receive the GI Bill: In order to receive the GI Bill, your children must meet certain eligibility requirements, such as being a dependent child of a military member or Veteran. If they do not meet these requirements, they will not be able to use the GI Bill.
- Your children may not be able to use the GI Bill for certain types of education or training: Depending on the version of the GI Bill they are using, your children may not be able to use the benefit for certain types of education or training, such as online programs or non-degree programs.
- You may find yourself in a situation where you need additional training to pursue or advance in your next career.

Overall, transferring your GI Bill to your children can help them pay for their education and build successful careers. However, it is important to consider the potential drawbacks and make sure that transferring the GI Bill is the right decision for you and your family.

The value of the Post-9/11 GI Bill depends on several factors, including the length of time you served on active duty, the type of education or training you are pursuing, and the location of your school. However, here are some general estimates of the maximum benefits you may be able to receive under the Post-9/11 GI Bill:

- **Tuition and fees:** The GI Bill covers the cost of tuition and fees for in-state public schools and up to $24,476.79 per academic year for private schools or out-of-state public schools. You can also look into the "Yellow Ribbon Program." Schools that enter into the Yellow Ribbon Program contribute to a student's tuition that is above the limits of the GI Bill; see more information here: https://www.va.gov/education/about-gi-bill-benefits/post-9-11/yellow-ribbon-program/
- **Monthly housing allowance:** This is based on the Department of Defense's Basic Allowance for Housing (BAH) rate for an E-5 with dependents and is paid to students who are attending school at least half-time. The monthly housing allowance will vary from location to location and state to state.
- **Books and supplies stipend:** This is a flat rate of up to $1,000 per academic year and is paid to students who are enrolled at least half-time.
- **Other benefits:** The GI Bill also covers the cost of certain types of education and training, such as vocational or technical training, apprenticeships, and on-the-job

training. The benefits you can receive for these programs depend on the length of your active-duty service and the type of training you are pursuing.

It's important to note that these estimates are subject to change and may not reflect the actual amount of benefits you will receive. In addition, the GI Bill also has some restrictions and limitations, such as a cap on the number of months of benefits you can receive, so it's a good idea to consult with the Department of Veterans Affairs (VA) or a VA-approved school to get a more accurate estimate of the benefits you may be eligible to receive.

Whatever school you go to, make sure the credits will transfer unless you are sure you can complete your degree program before you move.

Credentialling Opportunities On-Line (COOL) Programs:[xxxiii] Each branch of the Military Service (Army, Navy, Air Force, Marine Corps, Coast Guard) and DOD Civilians have their own COOL website, designed expressly for them. Each site contains resources and information on credentialing and the military. In addition, military members have access to some of the industry's best and most current training platforms through this tool.

Free Online Classes: Free universities like Udemy or the Khan Academy offer college-level courses completely free of charge. Although these courses do not offer you credit towards a degree, they provide students the opportunity to take courses that will help in their overall academic goals. For example, I recently registered for a free statistics course on Udemy in advance of a business class I am scheduled to take the following semester. I did this to improve my understanding of the subject and my chances of overall success.

Trade schools: In lieu of traditional education, trade schools offer education and training in some of the highest-paid civilian jobs. Many of these trades are closely related to or are the same as the work you may have done on active duty. For example, jobs such as Radiation Therapists, Nuclear Medicine Technologists, Dental Hygienists, Electrical and Electronics Engineering Technicians, Aircraft and Avionics Equipment Mechanics and Technicians, Boilermakers, Construction and Building Inspectors, and Electricians are just a sample of very lucrative careers that can be learned through trade schools.

Professional Certifications: The military offers many opportunities to obtain certifications that will transfer to your post-military life. All you have to do is determine what you want to do after the military and set your sights on being a certified professional in that field. During your transition from the military, you will have additional opportunities for free certification training and testing. Be sure to pay attention to the programs explained to you at the Transition Assistance Program (TAP). During that week, you will be introduced to organizations with money specifically set aside for you to get a professional certification.

The education described in this chapter may not get you a job, but not having any education after high school will likely prevent you from being paid what you are worth. Education is an easy discriminator. Some places will take experience in lieu of a degree, but you have to be able to get in the door first. In my experience, employers are attracted to candidates that have invested in themselves.

Money Pits

- Paying a ton for education only to discover your credits do not transfer to the final school that will award your degree.
- Paying for useless degrees. If you have to ask, you probably already know the answer.
- Attending non-accredited schools. The piece of paper they tell you is a degree isn't worth the cost of the paper it's printed on.
- Being forced to pay back tuition assistance for failing a class.
- Earning a professional certification only to let it lapse.

9

Medical Care

"To get rich, never risk your health. For it is the truth that health is the wealth of wealth."

~ Richard Baker

The military will take a lot from you; this is the sacrifice of service. For some during my generation, the wars in Afghanistan, Iraq, Syria, and North Africa took more than anyone should have to bear. Some have physical scars, while others wear invisible wounds. In those cases, and every other, I would say the same thing. You must be a demanding customer of your medical benefits.

It's important to understand why this chapter exists in a book about thriving on a military salary. It's because, beyond your time in service, another department of the government has a responsibility to you as long as you live. In fact, the Department of Veterans Affairs (VA) will be with you far longer than the DoD. Besides being your point of contact and servicing agency for the GI Bill and home loan guarantee benefits, the two most important things the VA does for you are to compensate you for disabilities linked to your active duty service and provide you with medical care, if eligible.

"All gave some, some gave all."

~ Billy Ray Cyrus

Don't skip this chapter. Right or wrong, the compensation you may be entitled to after your separation, in the form of a tax-free check for life, may be worth more than your retirement check after twenty years of service. When I arrived on this side of the uniform, I realized how I failed in my own personal medical responsibilities. I was the guy who would only go to the clinic when absolutely required to stay green for mobility status or to stay off the commander's 'failure to get a flu shot' list. For me, that extended to dental care too. I would go when required to avoid getting in trouble. The only clinic I went to consistently was optometry because my eyes suck, and I need corrective lenses to keep my shot group tight on target.

So yeah, I was late to the game when it came to medical. This chapter can be summarized into two points: 1) go to the doc and 2) make sure they write down why you were there and what caused it. Furthermore, don't fall into the trap of saving additional concerns for the last minute or two when the doctor asks, 'Is there anything else bothering you?' Lay it all out from the beginning. Those add-ons rarely, if ever, make your medical file. Be a demanding customer! It could be worth its own fortune upon separation. Want details? Keep reading.

If you are like me and lived your life suffering through pain, I am talking to you. Go get it checked and documented. The time to start is right now. If you are reading this and you are on your way to separating or retiring, be sure to get every concern you have looked at while you are still in uniform. Go see every clinic, even if you have never set foot in that clinic before. Often overlooked clinics like gastroenterology, ear, nose, and throat, and the sleep clinic could uncover unknown ailments that may lead to later compensation. The military will perform all the tests to determine causes and prescribe treatments. This is free to you and much easier to complete while still on active duty. Regardless, the VA will use everything in your record to determine your disability rating. Disabled is a dumb word, and I wish it wasn't how the VA categorized medical complaints. Although you may not feel 'disabled,' you should never leave the military without making a VA claim. Just a few seemingly minor conditions could grant you lifelong access to VA medical care and potentially supplemental income. The Disabled American Veterans (DAV) has an office on or near every major installation. Their counselors will help review your record before you submit your claim to the VA.

Additional nonprofits can also guide you along this process. I can personally vouch for the Wounded Warrior Project.

While you are still in the military, you should always prioritize free access to care and medical procedures that are very costly off-base. Procedures like corrective eye surgery or complex dental work should always be done while you are still in uniform. There is no reason to wait until you get out and be forced to pay deductibles and copays.

There are other ways to save money when it comes to your health. They include:

Medication

- Always use free on-base pharmacies.
- Don't pay for over-the-counter medicine that you can get prescribed and given for free.
- Only as a last resort, co-pay at local pharmacies.

Vision

- Get your annual eye exams and update your glasses and contact lenses prescription.
- Always choose the two pairs of glasses that are provided for free, even if you don't plan to use them.

- If eligible, apply for corrective eye surgery. If it's not offered near you, your local optometrist can help you with the process to get the procedure done at a provided facility.

Dental

- Get your annual exams and cleaning.
- Request a night guard and sports guard.
- Stay current on all X-rays.
- Ensure all cavities receive fillings.
- If applicable, get your wisdom teeth removed.
- If applicable, complete all advanced treatments (crowns, braces, etc.) before separating.

Mental Health

- For family issues, attend sessions at your local family support center.
- For personal concerns, go to the behavioral health clinic.
- Chaplains can be a great resource to talk through issues.
- Off-base free options exist for active duty members like Military One Source, www.militaryonesource.mil.

Once you are out of the military, there are many healthcare options. For those that are separated, the most common method is to get coverage through your new employer. For those not looking to jump right into the job market, The Affordable Care Act (ACA) offers relatively inexpensive preventable medicine. Prevention is easier and cheaper than corrective medicine. Whatever you choose, make sure you keep up with your health, including an annual physical, dental exam/cleaning, and vision check, at a minimum.

If you retired from active duty, you have some additional options, including:[xxxiv]

- **TRICARE Select:** This will cost you a little more out of pocket, but you get to pick your providers and do not need referrals for any clinic.
- **TRICARE Prime:** Offers a lower out-of-pocket rate, but you will continue to go through the military hospital/clinic for treatment and all your referrals.

As stated earlier, the cost of TRICARE is extremely low compared to third-party civilian insurance. This also gives you an advantage when securing civilian employment. By opting out of an employer-provided plan, you may be able to negotiate a higher salary.

Lastly, TRICARE also offers inexpensive family plans that may be a good fit for your family.

Money Pits

- Waiting to get known medical conditions in your medical records.
- Waiting to get out to get medical procedures done.
- Failing to file a VA disability claim.
- Not securing health, dental, and vision insurance after separation or retirement.

10

Benefits and Discounts

"Great grace and small gifts are better than great gifts and no grace."

~ John Bunyan

I'm cheap. If I can get a nickel off a one-dollar chicken sandwich, I'll take it. In my mind (and in reality), those nickels add up. It doesn't matter if I need more money or not. I will always chase a discount. I will also drive to the base on a Saturday to buy something and save sales tax. If there is a website that uses ID.me to give me a discount based on my military service, I'm on it. Even if a company doesn't outwardly offer a military discount, I'll call their corporate headquarters and ask. Most of the time, they will extend some discount off the regular price. Bottom line, I like my money in my pocket, not someone else's. When you go into every transaction knowing that you aren't going to pay the advertised price, it becomes a powerful habit. In the few instances where you are forced to pay the advertised price, you will have given yourself one additional chance to weigh the purchase in your head and one more chance to opt out. These habits, built over time, are more powerful than those saved nickels. You will be on your way to financial freedom.

I am aware that this chapter can act as a double-edged sword. The intent of including it in this book is to save you money. I am keenly aware that by highlighting some of these deals, the shop-a-holic in you may be drawn to go and check out these sweet hook-ups and inspire you to spend money you would otherwise not have spent. Don't do it! Let your civilian counterparts spend themselves into poverty. There is no reason you suddenly 'need' something just because you read this chapter. If you require a reminder about the pitfalls of consumer goods, go back and reread Chapter 3 before continuing. For those of you wanting to learn how to stretch your money by utilizing your military benefits and discounts, continue reading. This chapter identifies several well-known and some lesser-known benefits and perks to keeping more money in your pocket.

On Base Services/Shopping:

Multiple shops and services are offered on base, either free or at reduced costs.

- **Gym:** The average cost of a gym membership is between $600-$900.[xxxv] You get access to gyms for free. There are also running tracks and indoor/outdoor pools. With the rise in popularity of cross fit, more outdoor cross fit gyms and apparatuses are appearing on posts all the time.

- **Outdoor Recreation:** Many installations provide low-cost outdoor equipment rentals (e.g., ski/snowboard equipment, camping gear, and sometimes boats and campers).
- **Tickets and Tours:** Provides discounted tickets for many local attractions and major national attractions (i.e., Disney, Universal Studios, etc.)
- **Base Theater:** It might not be as fancy as the off-base theaters, but the movies are first run, the popcorn is hot, and the price is much lower. If you have children, this is an inexpensive reprieve.
- **Judge Advocate General (JAG):** On base/post, you can access free legal counsel. Be sure to use this service to create your Will, Living Will, and Power of Attorney (if/when you deploy).
- **Base Exchange/Post Exchange/Navy Exchange (BX/PX/NEX):** The most significant advantage to shopping on base is no sales tax. This can make a massive difference if you buy large appliances or computers, and the crowds are smaller if you are trying to finish your Christmas shopping without losing your mind.
- **Commissary:** The goal of the commissary is to save you at least 25% on your groceries. Don't let anyone tell you

that tipping the baggers and the surcharge overcomes the savings. The prices are constantly measured against the economy, and across nearly all food items, you will save money. As an added bonus, they also carry pet food.[xxxvi]

- **Package Store/Class 6:** You can buy alcohol, mixers, and supplies here. It also carries items normally found in a Shopette.
- **Auto Hobby Shop:** Many bases/posts have a place that provides room and equipment to work on your own vehicles. Most, if not all, employ at least one ASE (Automotive Service Excellence) certified master mechanic, and you can get some of your routine maintenance done for significantly less than off base. Even if they do not offer full-service maintenance (oil changes, tire balancing, etc.), the mechanics that work there are almost always willing to help or, at the very least, teach you. The lessons you learn in the auto hobby shop can translate to hundreds or thousands of dollars over your life. For example, a simple brake job...is precisely that... simple. On one of my previous cars, the cost for the dealership to replace the front and rear pads and wear sensors was nearly $1,000. I was able to purchase the parts and do the labor myself for a total of $230.
- **Frame Shop:** Framing, plaques, and related items that rival the cost at big box stores and usually include customization in the cost of the item.

- **Thrift Shop:** Most bases/posts have a consignment shop on base that will sell your unwanted items for you. It is also a great place to find low-cost household items and clothing.
- **Library:** Books, movies, and video games can be checked out all at no charge. Libraries are constantly evolving and expanding their offerings. In some instances, I've seen where day passes to parks and museums can be checked out. Some libraries are now offering 3D printers and recording studios.
- **Housing Office:** When you move to a new area, the Housing Office can advise you about the good and bad areas to live. They can help with finding rental properties. This is also where you will go in order to get on the base housing list. In lower-demand markets, as a retiree, you may be able to rent and live on the base where a contracted company operates the housing.

Other Discounts:

- **Microsoft Workplace Discount Program:** (formerly the Home Use Program (HUP)) This program allows you to purchase single copies of Microsoft programs at greatly discounted prices. For more information, go to www.microsoft.com/en-us/workplace-discount-program.

- **Anti-Virus:** The DoD antivirus software license allows DoD employees and authorized government contractors to utilize McAfee free for one year.[xxxvii]

Many businesses, especially in towns that host a military installation, offer military discounts (usually around 10%). Not all of them advertise it, so don't forget to ask at:

- Restaurants
- Big Box Hardware stores (e.g., Ace, Lowes, and Home Depot)
- Hotels (Government Rate)
- Cell Phones (ATT / Verizon / T-Mobile)
- Airlines

"It never hurts to ask."

~ Unknown

This is just scratching the surface of military discounts. There are too many to list here. To help you, the following sites contain lists of corporations providing military discounts. Be advised some stores require you to register beforehand (e.g., online) to receive the discounts.

- www.veteransadvantage.com/
- https://themilitarywallet.com/military-discounts/
- www.dealnews.com/features/discounts/military-discounts/
- www.govx.com/
- www.sheerid.com/shoppers/militarydeals/
- www.military.com/discounts

11

Access to Cash

"There are no downsides to a side hustle. There are only benefits to building more than one source of income."

~ Forbes

No plan survives first contact. You may have a budget, substantial savings, and strategy, but then life happens. Emergencies and accidents are unplanned, unforeseen, and inescapable. The fact is, anything can be an emergency when it comes to facing a huge bill that 'must' be paid now. I understand that everyone reading this book may not have an emergency fund. It's essential to arm you with information on how to access cash right now so you don't do something stupid like liquidate your assets or take a considerable cash advance from your credit cards.

When I was in my twenties and thirties, I was financially illiterate. Every month I would make it rain for five days after every paycheck, then transition back to ramen until the next payday. It was a dangerous game of roulette. It was fun, but I was wasting valuable time that could have been spent amassing a fortune. One winter, I was renting a house in Colorado when a water line blew on the side of the house. It must have been spewing water for at least a day before I realized it. Apparently, it's a high-failure item, especially if you don't winterize your sprinkler system. I didn't know that was a thing. An ounce of prevention could have saved me hundreds of dollars. Instead, I had to pay an emergency plumber to come out on a Sunday. That was a credit card expense I was not planning for. I put myself in a bad spot because I failed to plan, and my go-to move then was to keep on sucking at life. At the time, I wasn't making a lot of money and didn't know how to pay off the additional expense and the added interest. I was lucky at the time that I had a card available that wasn't maxed out.

This story is easy to identify with because it could happen to anyone. For some with lousy luck, stuff like this follows you around like a black cloud. The worst thing to do when you are in a hole is to keep digging. This chapter will explain some ways to get access to cash right now. You do not have to pawn your ring or sell a kidney on the dark web. There are agencies that understand the challenges you are facing, and they are run by amazing people who do not want you to fail. If you are in a rut and need cash now, keep reading. For everyone else, pay it forward by learning about these organizations and teaching your troops so that their entire financial future isn't set back or ruined by an unfortunate expense.

The best time to save money is when you have it. First things first, look at cutting expenses to create an emergency fund. As a standard rule, I tell people to have access to $10k. Although that amount may seem high to some, it may not seem like enough to others. This money is for emergencies only. Emergency expenditures are those times considered 'must pay' instances. There are far less real emergencies than you may think. If you are in the animal ER or your only vehicle is currently sitting on the back of a tow truck, you are experiencing a real financial emergency. I'm talking about expenses that are so mandatory that you cannot go to bed without giving someone else a sum of money to move to the next hour of your life. Tickets to Coachella or Burning Man are not emergency expenses.

Supplement Your Income

Whether to make ends meet or to save up for something special, there are many ways that someone could supplement their income:

- **Freelance or gig work:** One way to supplement your income is to take on freelance or gig work in your field of expertise or in a related area. This could include writing, editing, web design, graphic design, photography, online influencing, or consulting.

- **Rent out a room on a Short-Term Rental site:** If you have a spare room in your home, you could rent it out to travelers looking for short-term accommodations. The likelihood a serial killer chooses to rent your room is statistically very low.
- **Ride Share or Food Delivery Driver:** Both of these are managed online and allow you to work as needed and on your own schedule.
- **Sell items (Garage Sale, Consignment Store, Flea Market, Online):** If you have things that you no longer need or use, you could sell them on eBay or Etsy to make some extra money.
- **Rent out your car:** If you have a vehicle that you don't use all the time, you can rent it out via online apps to people who need a car for a day or longer. Check with your insurance first to avoid any unpleasant surprises.
- **Participate in paid focus groups or surveys:** There are many companies that conduct focus groups or surveys and are willing to pay for people's opinions. You can find opportunities to participate in these types of studies online or through market research firms.
- **Offer your services as a tutor or teacher:** If you have a particular skill or subject matter expertise, you could offer your services as a tutor or teacher to students in your area.

- **Rent out your equipment or tools:** If you have equipment or tools you don't use all the time, you could rent them out to people in your community who need them for a project or task.
- **Do odd jobs for people in your neighborhood:** You could offer to do odd jobs for people in your neighborhood or around the area, such as mowing lawns, shoveling snow, or doing simple maintenance tasks.
- **Sell homemade products or crafts:** If you have a talent for making things, you could sell your homemade products or crafts online or at local craft fairs or markets.
- **Online Editing:** Freelance editors can get paid between $0.015 and $0.028 per word. It is usually done by the word vs. hours because better editors can go faster.[xxxviii]

  It can be lucrative if you have the time, skill, and inclination.

"Sometimes asking for help is the bravest move you can make. You don't have to go it alone."

~ Liz Lamoreux

If you take a part-time job, ensure it does not interfere with your military service and notify your chain of command (and legal office if required). The additional benefit of working more is that it usually equates to spending less.

Digging Out of a Hole.

There are a few options you can consider if you need to access money in a bind:

- **Borrow from friends or family:** This is usually the first option people consider because it is often the easiest and quickest way to get the money you need. However, it is important to remember to treat this as a loan and make a plan to pay the money back.
- **Take out a loan:** There are several types of loans available, such as personal loans, home equity, debt consolidation, title, cash advance, and payday loans. Personal loans and payday loans are generally unsecured, meaning you do not need to put up collateral. The title of your vehicle secures title loans. Remember that taking out a loan can be expensive, especially if you have a low credit score, so be sure to compare rates and read the fine print before committing to a loan. Stay away from cash advances and payday loans. Their interest rates are too high, and many of the businesses offering them have been blacklisted by the military.
- **Sell possessions:** If you have items that you no longer need or use, you may be able to sell them to get the money you need. You can sell things online through platforms

like eBay or Facebook Marketplace, or you can sell them locally through classified ads or garage sales.

- **Get a part-time job:** If you have some extra time, you may be able to pick up a part-time job to bring in some extra money. There are many websites and apps that can help you find gig work or temporary positions in your area.
- **Consider government assistance:** If you are struggling to make ends meet, you may be able to get help from the government. This can include programs like SNAP (Supplemental Nutrition Assistance Program) or TANF (Temporary Assistance for Needy Families). There is absolutely no shame in utilizing programs that are meant to support you. In many cases, the taxes you are already paying go to support these programs. Never, never, never put your future self at financial risk because you are too proud in the present to utilize social resources. Once you understand this point, you can break the generational poverty cycle.
- **Military Relief Organizations:** Your military service relief organization can assist you with serious financial problems. For example, Army Emergency Relief, the Navy-Marine Corps Relief Society, the Air Force Aid Society, and Coast Guard Mutual Assistance may be able to help with interest-free loans, grants, or a combination of loans and grants. They can also offer financial

preparedness counseling and tuition assistance. Visit your Military Service relief organization's website to learn more about eligibility and how to apply for aid. https://www.defense.gov/Resources/Military-Support-Organizations/.

Be sure to contact your first sergeant (or equivalent) for further information, especially for government assistance or to access military relief organizations.

Promotion/Bonus/Extra Cash.

Getting a bonus at work can be an excellent opportunity to improve your financial situation, but making intelligent decisions with the extra money is important. Here are a few ideas for how to use a bonus:

"People don't get promoted for doing their jobs really well. They get promoted by demonstrating their potential to do more."

~ Tara Jaye Frank

- **Pay off high-interest debt:** If you have credit card debt or other high-interest loans, using your bonus to pay them off can save you a significant amount of money in the long run. However, paying off lower balances first and then using that payment on the next card/loan is more beneficial. This practice is called the debt snowball method.

- **Build up your emergency fund:** Having an emergency fund can provide a financial cushion in case of unexpected expenses or income loss. Consider using your bonus to build up your emergency fund to a sufficient level. I recommend $10k.
- **Save for the future:** If you don't have any pressing financial needs, you might consider saving your bonus for the future. This could include contributing to a retirement account, saving for a down payment on a house, or building up your investment portfolio.
- **Invest in your career:** If you have wanted to take a professional development course or get a certification that could improve your job prospects or earning potential, you could use your bonus to invest in your career. Be sure to look for free options first and only pay out of pocket as a last resort.
- **Treat yourself:** It's okay to use some of your bonus to indulge in a little something special, whether it's a nice meal out, a new gadget, or a fun experience. Just be sure to balance the fun stuff with more practical, long-term financial decisions. Most bonuses come with some sort of timeline associated with them. It would be best if you always made it a goal to make that money last or grow for as long as the term it was earned. For example, if you received a re-enlistment bonus in exchange for four additional years of service, the bonus should last you or grow to a more significant amount over those four years,

at minimum. Of course, that can only happen if you start saving it before you are used to having it.

- **Buy assets:** Use the bonus to buy something that can generate more money for you. If you drive a truck, buying a snowplow for the front would allow you to pick up additional income. Good at cutting hair? Buy a new set of clippers to keep those fades fresh and your pockets filled with cash.

Money Pits

- Allowing your personal pride to keep you from applying for/receiving subsistence.
- Spending a bonus or influx of cash before you actually get it.
- Failing to establish an emergency fund and bailing yourself out with credit.
- Participating in Multilevel Marketing (MLM). Don't do it. These 'companies' sell products or services person-to-person through your social network. These people prey on the military, especially spouses. You know them, those who are selling candles, vitamins, CBD, or lingerie/personal massagers at hosted parties. It will cost you more money than you will ever make. Do not do it! These people are complete scammers.

12

Budgeting

"A budget is telling your money where to go instead of wondering where it went."

~ Dave Ramsey

If I made one good decision in my adult life, it was cheating off of someone else's work. As awful as that sounds, it's the truth. I'll go even further to say I am offering you to cheat off mine now. What am I talking about? A budget. I have an aunt that I would hang out with a lot because she lived close to where I went to school, plus she would usually feed me. She was always messing with this spreadsheet on Microsoft Excel. This was when Excel was still pretty new, at least to me. She was constantly tweaking it and adjusting numbers in the cells. I finally asked her why she spent so much time messing with it. She told me she made more money messing with that spreadsheet than doing anything else. That was the hook I needed. I asked her to show me how it worked, and she emailed me a copy. I erased her data and replaced it with my own. I have used the same budget now for over twenty years. Stealing my aunt's budget has made me more money than anything I have ever created, including this book.

I equate a budget to a playbook. When you are a kid at recess and play two-hand touch, the plays look the same; everyone goes long and hopes to catch a touchdown. When you start playing at a higher level in high school, college, or professionally, the players have a playbook. In that playbook, there are specific assignments for each player. If the play is executed well, yards are effectively gained or defended. Even if things don't go perfectly in one play, there are other plays that are put in place and a strategy to follow. Imagine if two professional teams played against each other and only one had a playbook while the other played without one. It's easy to see how much of an advantage the team with the playbook would have over the other. That is the same as choosing to budget versus spending your income without a plan.

In this chapter, we will break down a simple budget. This is easy. Budgeting is the most critical thing you can do for your present quality of life and financial future. If you don't have a plan for every dollar you have coming in, rest assured it will find its own destination and won't be to build you long-term wealth.

Creating and maintaining a budget is an essential part of managing your finances and achieving your financial goals. A budget is a plan for how you will allocate your income and expenses over a given period, and it can help you take control of your money and make the most of it. There are several reasons why creating and maintaining a budget is so important.

- **A budget helps you track your spending:** With a budget, it can be easy to keep track of where your money is going. By creating a budget, you can see exactly how much money you have coming in and going out each month, and you can identify areas where you may be able to cut back or save more.
- **A budget helps you set financial goals:** A budget can help you clarify your financial goals and plan how to achieve them. Whether you want to save for a down payment on a house, pay off credit card debt, or build up your emergency fund, a budget can help you to see what you need to do to reach your goals.
- **A budget helps you to prioritize your spending:** With a budget, you can decide what is most important to you and allocate your money accordingly. This can help you avoid overspending on unnecessary items and make sure you spend your money on things that truly matter to you.
- **A budget can help you save money:** By tracking your spending and identifying areas where you can cut back, a budget can help you save money. This can be especially

helpful if you are trying to pay off debt or build up your emergency fund.

- **A budget can help you avoid financial stress:** Managing your money can be stressful, especially if you feel like you don't have a handle on your finances. By creating a budget, you can take control of your money and reduce financial stress by removing the emotion.

Creating and maintaining a budget is important in managing your finances and achieving your financial goals. It can help you track your spending, set financial goals, prioritize your spending, save money, and avoid financial stress. In addition, making a budget a part of your regular financial routine allows you to set yourself up for long-term financial success.

"He who fails to plan is planning to fail."

~ Winston Churchill

One thing to keep in mind as you make your budget is to always **pay yourself first**. This encourages setting aside money for things like retirement, savings, and debt before paying for other variable expenses.[xxxix]

In the budget on the following page, the person earns $3,250 per month and spends $2,715 per month, leaving them with $535 of extra income. They allocate some of this extra income towards retirement and emergency fund savings. This budget is just a sample and can be adjusted based on individual circumstances and financial goals, but it is offered for those who need help knowing where to begin.

Money Pits

- Failing to establish a budget.
- Having a budget and not following it to the letter.
- Allowing short-term wants to outweigh your long-term goals.

Here's a sample budget for a single person that has put some of the recommendations from this book into action:

Monthly Income:	
Total pay after deductions:	$3,000
Side hustle income:	$250
Total Monthly Income:	$3,250
Monthly Expenses:	
Rent:	$1,200
Utilities:	$150
Internet/Cable:	$80
Cell phone:	$60
Groceries:	$300
Eating out:	$100
Gas/Transportation:	$150
Entertainment:	$50
Clothing:	$50
Personal care:	$30
Car insurance:	$100
Renters insurance:	$20
Retirement savings:	$325
Emergency fund savings:	$100
Total Monthly Expenses:	$2,715
Remaining Income:	$535

13

(Bad) Debt

"Bad debt is sacrificing your future day needs for your present-day desires."

~ Suze Orman

Debt is amazing. It's the ability to take something today for the promise that sometime in the future, you will pay full value (or drastically more) for the item or service you have already enjoyed. What's not to love? Debt and credit will be used interchangeably in this chapter. Both will mean that you have spent it on a good or service but still owe for it for some determined amount of time. When I first started out, I was told I had to have a Military Star Card. I was also told I needed a club card for the club on base. Credit cards find a way of finding you when you are in the military. The promise of a paycheck on time twice a month keeps you telling yourself it will all be okay.

I signed up for my first credit card when I was 16 years old. It was a store credit card for a place at the mall. I was required to sign up because I was hired to fold shirts there one summer in high school. That went as bad as it could have. After a few months, I was fired from that job for charging a bread maker on the card. Apparently, the loss prevention people thought that I was suspicious and I must have been misusing my employee card because 'Hey, why does a 16-year-old need a bread maker?' It was a gift for my aunt. I hated that job.

The next 'real' credit card I applied for, I remember distinctly signing up because the people called me over and offered me a free t-shirt on the spot for signing up. Little did I know that I was opening up Pandora's box. I had not learned about credit scores, credit card limits, or interest rates. I also had never heard of budgeting. (Budgeting is discussed in detail in Chapter 12.) At the time, I thought I could get whatever I wanted, and a bill would come in the mail the next month. I would write a check for a small portion of what was owed, and I would do that forever. I was 'adulting.' The problem was that it only works if there is money in a checking account somewhere that can cover the checks you are writing.

It's a memorable line from the first Top Gun movie, when Captain Tom "Stinger" Jordan tells "Maverick," "Your ego is writing checks your body can't cash." Unfortunately, that was true for me, and I can imagine it's true for some of you too. The greatest strength of serving in the military, financially speaking, is the financial security of two paychecks a month and, at minimum, annual raises. It's also our greatest risk of financial ruin. This chapter will focus on bad debt and provide some education and insight into the common traps. This will contrast with the next chapter, where we will talk about good debt, those instances when borrowed money is growing your wealth as an appreciating asset.

If you, like me, have maxed out cards, bought furniture on same-as-cash, or ever had something repossessed as I have, keep reading.

According to Investopedia, Good Debt/Bad Debt are defined as follows:[xl]

> *"Not all debts are equal. Good debt has the potential to increase your wealth, while bad debt costs you money with high interest on purchases for depreciating assets.*
>
> *Determining whether a debt is good or bad sometimes depends on an individual's financial situation, including how much they can afford to lose."*

A great example many young military members make is buying clothes and food on credit. If you can't pay the credit card off in full every month, you could be paying for that pizza you ate in five minutes ten years later. Unfortunately, almost all bad debt looks and feels the same. It's a balance hanging over your head and a monthly bill asking you to pay a minimum payment while the balance grows through interest by 18-29%. Have you ever read the details of your credit card statements? One example I saw recently, a credit card balance of $6500 will take seventeen years to pay off if you make just the minimum payments!

There are better ways to achieve financial freedom. Financial problems can quickly find their way into your professional life if your debt starts to overcome your repayment efforts. If you have a security clearance, be sure to notify your chain of command and security office if you are having financial difficulties. Being proactive will demonstrate responsibility and likely save your clearance. Be prepared to describe your plan to get out of debt.

Here are some ways to eliminate bad debt:

- **Create a budget:** The first step to eliminating debt is to get a handle on your spending and figure out where your money is going. By creating a budget, you can see exactly how much money you have coming in and going out each month, and you can identify areas where you may be overspending.
- **Stop using credit cards:** Credit cards can be a convenient way to pay for things, but they can also lead

to debt if you aren't careful. Try using cash or a debit card instead to reduce your reliance on credit cards.

- **Pay more than the minimum payment:** If you only make the minimum payment on your credit card balances each month, it will take you much longer to pay off your debt, and you will end up paying more in interest. Instead, try to pay as much as you can each month to pay off your debt more quickly.
- **Use a debt snowball or debt avalanche method:** The debt snowball method involves paying off your debts from smallest to largest. In contrast, the debt avalanche method involves paying off your debts with the highest interest rates first. Both of these strategies can help you pay off your debt more quickly and save money on interest.
- **Negotiate with your creditors:** If you are having trouble making your payments, you may be able to negotiate a lower interest rate or a payment plan with your creditors.
- **Debt Consolidation Loans:** These roll your debt into a single loan payment, making paying simpler. The rate may or may not be lower, and there could be up-front costs. There are other potential negative consequences, like damage to your credit score.
- **Home Equity Line Of Credit (HELOC):**[xli] These are just as dangerous as a credit card. The interest rate is

calculated just like a credit card. Despite being a tool to access cash, using a HELOC to pay off bad debt rolls that debt into your most valuable asset, your home. This is almost never a good move.

- **Seek help from a credit counselor:** If you are struggling to manage your debt, you may benefit from working with a credit counselor who can help you create a budget, negotiate with your creditors, and come up with a plan to pay off your debt. Credit counselors can be good, however, if they are the ones who pay off your bills and charge you a monthly rate, run like hell. Credit services can kill your credit, can be expensive, and can leave you in worse shape than before you went to them.
- **Consider bankruptcy as a last resort:** If you cannot pay off your debt and your creditors are unwilling to work with you, you may need to consider filing for bankruptcy. This should be a last resort, as bankruptcy can have serious consequences and may not be the right choice for everyone. Your credit is flagged for ten years, which will affect your ability to get loans.
- **Build an emergency fund:** It's important to build an emergency fund to help you avoid falling into debt again in the future. Aim to save approximately $10k or enough money to cover three to six months' worth of living expenses in case of unexpected expenses or a loss of income.

- **Practice good financial habits:** To avoid falling into debt again, it's important to practice good financial habits, such as living within your means, paying your bills on time, and saving for the future. Being proactive about your finances can set you up for long-term financial success.

Here's the issue. The military is in the credit card game and brings you along. The government travel card is mandatory for most people and is intended to be used for official travel only. Your club card may give you a dollar off of bowling or two dollars off of your burger, but it is just another credit card. Finally, the PX/BX pushes the STAR card. You are already getting the items tax-free. Leave the Star Card alone. This, too, is a credit card and counts against your credit rating. None of these people are helping you by giving you credit cards for your benefit. They are pushing them because they know they will get paid.

Money Pits

- These days, all credit cards are high-interest credit cards. Don't apply for them, and don't use them. They will not grow your wealth.
- Cash advance and payday advance loans.
- Not paying off "Same as Cash" loans before the deadline. You will pay all the accumulated interest.

- Chasing credit cards for points. If you are not level expert and have sizable savings, don't do it.
- Kiting- Paying off one credit card with another. Not only is this moving the problem rather than fixing it, but it may also actually tear the fabric of space-time.

14

(Good) Debt

"Not all debt is bad. From time to time we should get into debt when there is a good reason for that."

~ Dan Ariely

Believe it or not, leveraging "Good Debt" to accumulate long-term wealth can make you rich beyond your imagination. Before Dave Ramsey accuses me of being a menace to society, I will qualify my statement. Using debt to amass assets that cover their own expense, provide adequate holdbacks, and still have some profit left over is how many people accumulate huge amounts of wealth. It's called capitalism. This is not as complicated as it seems. You must piece together only a few factors to make 1+1=16. The military provides you with a few amazing and free ways to quickly (relatively) amass money. In this chapter, we will discuss the purchase of assets that make you money. These items can range from rental properties, machinery, inventory, and in some cases, vehicles.

Good debt and a good credit score are things that should be managed intentionally by everyone in the military. I know many people who separated or retired from the military and are living extremely fulfilling lives. They no longer trade time for money. Assets generate money when you sleep, are on vacation, and even Monday through Friday during business hours. As soon as possible, I recommend implementing your plan for financial freedom. For many of us, that means buying assets.

Truth be told, I did not start buying assets until more than ten years into my career. I had invested, but nothing outside of TSP. In the last ten years of my career, I prioritized investing and put my accumulation of assets into overdrive. I started by asking a question. Could I make enough money through passive income to make up for the pay I would lose upon retirement?

I looked at my Leave and Earning Statement (LES) and found my base pay, housing allowance, and subsistence allowance. This amounted to my total take home pay.

Then I saw how much I was paying in federal taxes. I subtracted that number from my total take home pay.

Finally, I subtracted the estimated amount of monthly retirement pay I would receive by simply dividing my current base pay by 2. This was an estimate, but it would give me a very close answer to how much I would need to make the same amount of money monthly. Since I intentionally eliminated debt prior to retirement, the amount I was making monthly allowed me to live comfortably. I knew I could enjoy life indefinitely on this amount of monthly income. The best part, I would make the same take home pay for absolutely no time commitment, leaving me every single day to do things that fulfilled me. This became my financial goal.

Here are my calculations as an example:

Step 1. $12000.00 - $2530.00 = $9470.00

(Total Take Home Pay - Taxes 18% = Active Duty Net Pay)

Step 2. $9470.00 / 2 = $4735.00

(Active Duty Net Pay / 2 = Estimated Retirement Pay)

Step 3. $4735.00 – 18% = $3882.70

(Estimated Retirement Pay - Taxes 18% = Retirement Net Pay Estimate)

Step 4. $9470.00 – $3882.70 = $5587.30

(Active Duty Net Pay - Retirement Net Pay Estimate = My Goal Passive Income)

Answer. I would need to make about $5590.00 monthly in cash-flowing assets to be financially free by my retirement date.

If you can live on your current pay, you need to only make up for ½ base pay + BAH + BAS. For most people retiring at twenty years, you need to come up with $4-6k a month to break even (less than $34/hr).

If you want to be free of trading your time for money, you should consider using good debt to accumulate assets and fast-forward your retirement plan.

Many people associate the word debt with financial burdens and poor money management, but not all debt is created equal. Good debt, when managed responsibly, can be a powerful tool for accumulating long-term wealth. This chapter will explore various types of good debt, how they can help you build wealth, and the strategies you need to employ to make them work in your favor. In your case, military service has advantages that your civilian counterparts don't have.

Good debt is generally defined as debt that is used to finance assets that appreciate in value over time or generate income. This type of debt can be beneficial for your long-term financial health, as it can lead to a net increase in your wealth. Common examples of good debt include:

- Mortgages for primary residences and investment properties.

- Student loans to pursue higher education.
- Business loans to finance growth and expansion.
- Personal loans for investments or assets with growth potential.

A mortgage is a loan used to purchase real estate, and it is often considered one of the best types of good debt. Real estate has historically been a reliable long-term investment, with property values generally increasing over time. As a Service Member, you have access to the VA home loan guarantee. This benefit can be used on one house at a time (your primary residence, see VA.gov for additional exceptions) and can be your greatest access to wealth. By purchasing homes with the VA loan with little to no down payment, one can buy houses to amass assets, then reuse the benefit after refinancing into a traditional mortgage as early as six months after every purchase.

By using a mortgage to buy a home, you can:

- **Build equity:** As you pay down your mortgage and your property appreciates in value, your equity—the difference between your home's value and your outstanding loan balance—increases.
- **Leverage tax advantages:** Mortgage interest and property taxes are often tax-deductible, which can lower your overall tax burden.

- **Generate rental income:** If you invest in rental properties, you can earn passive income through monthly rent payments for tenants.

Education is another example of good debt, as it can lead to higher earning potential over your lifetime. By investing in your education through student loans or, better yet, using your GI Bill education benefits rather than passing it to your children, you can:

- **Increase your earning potential:** Higher education degrees often lead to better job opportunities and higher salaries.
- **Develop valuable skills:** Acquiring specialized knowledge and skill can make you more marketable in the job market and boost your long-term career prospects.
- **Generate additional passive income:** The Post 9-11 GI Bill will pay $90k on average in housing allowance over 36 months.

Business loans can help entrepreneurs and business owners finance growth, expansion, or business improvements. By taking on business debt, you can:

- **Grow your business:** Access to capital can help you invest in new equipment, facilities, or marketing efforts, potentially increasing revenue and profits.
- **Create jobs:** As your business grows, you may need to hire additional employees, which can contribute to your local economy and your personal wealth.

Personal loans can also be considered good debt if used strategically for investments or assets with growth potential. For example:

- **Investing in stocks, bonds, or mutual funds:** Personal loans can be used to finance investments that can generate returns over time, contributing to long-term wealth accumulation.
- **Purchasing assets that appreciate:** Buying assets such as artwork, collectibles, or classic cars can be a way to build wealth if they appreciate in value over time.

To make the most of good debt, it's essential to manage it responsibly. Here are some key strategies:

- **Borrow within your means:** Ensure that you can comfortably afford the monthly payments associated with any debt you take on, even better if the asset pays its own expenses.

- **Focus on appreciating or income-generating assets:** Prioritize investments with the potential for long-term growth or income generation.
- **Maintain a good credit score:** Good credit can help you secure better interest rates on loans, reducing the overall cost of borrowing. You can get up to three (one from each of the big three, Equifax, TransUnion, and Experian) free credit reports per year. Here are five ways to maintain a good credit score.[xlii]

    - Pay Your Bills on Time
    - Stay Below Your Credit Limit
    - Maintain Credit History With Older Credit
    - Apply for New Credit Only as Needed
    - Check Your Credit Reports for Errors

- **Refinance when appropriate:** Keep an eye on interest rates and consider refinancing your loans when it makes financial sense to do so.

Good debt, when managed wisely, can be a powerful tool for building long-term wealth. Any investments in assets should be carefully scrutinized and make sense to YOUR plan.

Pro Tip: Just because something may generate some level of long-term income doesn't mean it's necessarily right for you. We'd all love to own rare mineral rights on an asteroid, but that probably won't help your ability to build wealth in the next fifty years.

15

Investments

"If you wish to get rich, save what you get. A fool can earn money, but it takes a wise man to save and dispose of it to his own advantage."

~ Brigham Young

What would you do if money was not an object in your life? If you had no worries about how the bills would be paid, if you knew you had enough money to buy the dog toys forever, or if your kids didn't need to worry about braces, new shoes, or college debt? What would you do if money was not an issue?

As sad as it sounds, everyone in the military could be that person, and nearly all opt out. I know that may come as a surprise to many of you, especially if you are new to the military or have young children. Making a few hundred dollars a month is a far cry from being wealthy. I'm here to tell you, you have everything at your disposal now to stockpile a considerable sum of money. If you are an E1-5, I know how little you get paid. The struggle is real. I also know folks like you who are doing it for real. The secret is to pay your future self first. To refresh yourself on budgeting, revisit Chapter 12.

This chapter on investments will dive into the most common investment vehicles you have at your disposal right now. I'll break down the Thrift Savings Plan (TSP), Blended Retirement System (BRS), and Roth and Traditional Individual Retirement Accounts (IRAs). Next, we will look at real estate investment (REI), cryptocurrency, non-fungible tokens (NFTs), Certificates of Deposit (CDs), bonds, and precious metals. There really is a simple way to live well and grow wealth, but it can look different for everyone.

For me, I tried a little of everything. I put money into TSP, started a Roth IRA, bought some houses and a few bars of pure silver (for the apocalypse), and even bought some crypto (now tied up in litigation). Some worked well, while others tanked. Spoiler alert, it didn't matter. As I retired from active duty, I found myself in a position where I could do anything. My calling was to pay it forward and teach others how to get here. This chapter is important, so I hope you will choose to put it to work, and I look forward to seeing what you decide to do when *Money Ain't a Thang*. Shoutout to Jermaine Dupri!

The Thrift Savings Plan (TSP)[xliii] is a tax-deferred retirement savings plan that is available to military and federal employees. The TSP offers a range of investment options, including several index funds that are designed to match the performance of various stock and bond indices.

One of the key benefits of the TSP is its low administrative fees, which are significantly lower than those charged by most private-sector retirement plans. Additionally, TSP contributions are tax-deferred, meaning that the money is not subject to federal income tax until it is withdrawn during retirement.

To participate in the TSP, you simply contribute a portion of your salary up to the annual contribution limit set by the IRS. The TSP also offers a matching contribution of 1% for people under the Federal Employees Retirement System (for civilians), or 3% is matched dollar-for-dollar by your agency or service; the next 2% is matched at 50 cents on the dollar the Blended Retirement System (uniformed services).

In my opinion, the TSP is one of the world's most forgiving, lowest risk, and easiest investment tools available in the United States. I say that as I write this, in the winter of 2022, my TSP has lost nearly 30% of its total value from its all-time high. Yet, even now, it has proven to be my second most lucrative investment overall and the best return for how little time it took to maintain.

By that, I mean it took literally less than ten minutes a year to nudge my money between funds to chase economic trends. Moreover, the amount of personal time invested was near zero, while the gains over my career beat the stock market's 30-year average of 7.31%.

The Legacy Retirement System—also referred to as the Uniformed Services Retirement System—applies to Service Members who enlisted on or before December 31, 2017. This defined-benefit plan pays a lifetime monthly annuity to Service Members at retirement. You must have served for twenty years or longer to qualify for this benefit (some exceptions apply). Annuity payment amounts are based on the number of years of service and the average of the Service Member's highest 36 months of base pay.[xliv]

The Military Blended Retirement System (BRS)[xlv] is a retirement benefits program that was implemented by the Department of Defense in 2018. It is designed to provide retirement benefits to members of the military who joined the service on or after January 1, 2018, as well as to those who opted into the BRS during the opt-in period.

One of the key features of the BRS is that it combines a traditional defined benefit pension plan with a defined contribution plan, similar to a 401(k) plan. Under the BRS, military members can contribute to a TSP account, and the government will provide matching contributions of up to 5% of the member's base pay (see specific above).

Another important feature of the BRS is that it offers a mid-career continuation pay bonus to members who commit to serving an additional four years of active duty or six years in the Selected Reserve. This bonus can range from 2.5 to 13 times the member's monthly basic pay, depending on their branch of service and years of service.

Overall, the BRS is designed to provide a more flexible retirement benefits package for military members. By combining a traditional pension plan with a defined contribution plan and offering mid-career bonuses, the BRS seeks to provide a more equitable retirement benefits system that rewards Service Members for their dedication and commitment to the military.

Traditional and Roth IRAs are two popular types of individual retirement accounts that allow individuals to save for retirement in a tax-advantaged way.[xlvi]

A traditional IRA allows individuals to make contributions with pre-tax dollars, which means that contributions are tax-deductible in the year they are made. The money in the account grows tax-free until it is withdrawn during retirement, at which point it is taxed as ordinary income. Withdrawals before age fifty-nine and a half may be subject to a 10% early withdrawal penalty.

On the other hand, a Roth IRA allows individuals to make contributions with after-tax dollars, which means that contributions are not tax-deductible. However, the money in the account grows tax-free, and qualified withdrawals during retirement are also tax-free. Additionally, Roth IRAs do not require minimum distributions during the account holder's lifetime, unlike traditional IRAs.

One key difference between the two types of IRAs is their eligibility requirements. Traditional IRAs have no income limits for contributions, although contributions may not be tax-deductible for high earners who are covered by a workplace retirement plan. Roth IRAs, on the other hand, have income eligibility limits that determine how much an individual can contribute annually.

Overall, both traditional and Roth IRAs offer valuable tax advantages and can be powerful tools for retirement savings.

Real Estate Investing can be a viable option for individuals who are looking to save for retirement. There are plenty of books for real estate investors, but I've listed some of the most popular ways to invest in real estate for retirement:

- **Rental Properties:** Investing in rental properties can provide a steady stream of rental income that can be used to fund retirement expenses. Rental properties can appreciate in value over time, providing the potential for capital gains when sold.
- **Real Estate Investment Trusts (REITs):** A REIT is a company that owns and operates income-producing real estate properties. Investing in a REIT can provide exposure to the real estate market without the hassle of owning physical property. In addition, REITs typically pay out dividends to shareholders, which can be reinvested for additional growth.
- **Real Estate Crowdfunding:** Crowdfunding platforms allow investors to pool their money together to invest in real estate projects. This can be a good option for those who want to invest in real estate but need more capital or expertise to acquire and manage properties on their own.
- **Real Estate Mutual Funds:** Mutual funds that invest in real estate securities can provide exposure to a diversified portfolio of real estate assets. These funds can be a good option for those who want to invest in real estate but need more capital to buy property on their own.

Overall, investing in real estate can be a viable way to save for retirement. However, it's important to carefully evaluate each investment opportunity and consider factors such as risk, liquidity, and diversification before investing. Personally, I purchased primary residences at a few of my duty stations with the VA loan, which did not require a down payment. After living one year in a house, I refinanced into a traditional fixed-rate mortgage so I could reuse the VA loan at my next duty station. I would then rent the house when I moved to my next duty station. Once I had equity in three of these houses, I sold them and rolled the equity into fourteen lower-cost houses. This created a long-term passive income stream I enjoy today.

Cryptocurrency refers to digital or virtual currencies that use cryptography for security. Cryptocurrencies are decentralized and operate independently of a central bank or government, relying instead on blockchain technology to verify transactions and maintain a public ledger of all transactions. Examples of popular cryptocurrencies include Bitcoin, Ethereum, and Litecoin. Crypto can be bought and sold on cryptocurrency exchanges and can also be used as a form of payment for goods and services. While crypto has gained popularity in recent years, it is important to note that the market is highly volatile, and investing in cryptocurrency carries significant risks. However, there are potential benefits to including cryptocurrency in a retirement investment portfolio, including:

- **Diversification:** Adding cryptocurrency to a retirement portfolio can provide diversification, as it is a separate asset class from traditional stocks, bonds, and mutual funds. Diversification can help reduce overall portfolio risk.

- **Potential for high returns:** Cryptocurrency has the potential for high returns, as seen in the significant growth of Bitcoin and other digital currencies in recent years. However, it's important to remember that these gains are not guaranteed, and the market is highly volatile.
- **Decentralized and secure:** Cryptocurrency transactions are decentralized and secured through blockchain technology, which can provide greater security and transparency compared to traditional investments.
- **Tax benefits:** Some retirement accounts, such as self-directed IRAs, allow for investments in cryptocurrency. These accounts can provide tax benefits, such as tax-deferred growth and tax-free withdrawals during retirement.

Overall, investing in cryptocurrency for retirement can provide potential benefits, but evaluating the risks carefully is important. I dipped my toe in the crypto pond and at the time of this writing, it is tied up in litigation as the crypto exchange I used, Celsius, filed for bankruptcy. So, buyer beware, being on trend investment-wise usually isn't the path to wealth.

NFTs, or non-fungible tokens, are digital assets that represent ownership or proof of authenticity of a unique item or piece of content, such as art, music, videos, and other media files. Unlike cryptocurrencies such as Bitcoin or Ethereum, which are fungible and can be exchanged for one another, NFTs are unique and cannot be exchanged at a 1:1 ratio.

NFTs are built on blockchain technology, which provides a decentralized and transparent way to verify ownership and transfer of the asset. Once created, an NFT can be bought and sold on various online marketplaces using cryptocurrency.

The value of an NFT is determined by the market demand for the particular asset it represents. Some NFTs have sold for millions of dollars, such as a digital artwork by the artist, Beeple that sold for $69 million at a Christie's auction in 2021.[xlvii]

While NFTs have gained popularity in the art and entertainment industries, their long-term viability and impact on the broader economy remain unclear. However, as blockchain technology continues to evolve and more industries explore the potential uses of NFTs, they may become more mainstream in the future. In my opinion, I'm going to pass on these as a way to save for retirement.

A **Certificate of Deposit (CD)** is a type of savings account that typically offers a higher interest rate than a traditional savings account.[xlviii] CDs are designed to help people save money over a specific period of time, normally ranging from a few months to several years.

CDs can be an effective tool for retirement savings because they provide a guaranteed return on investment and are low risk. This means that you can be confident in the amount of money you will have at the end of the CD term, which can help you plan for retirement.

CDs are also FDIC-insured up to $250,000 per depositor, so your money is protected if the bank fails. This makes them a safe option for retirement savings.

One strategy for using CDs to save for retirement is to create a CD ladder. A CD ladder is a portfolio of CDs with varying maturity dates. For example, you might purchase a 1-year CD, a 2-year CD, a 3-year CD, and a 5-year CD. As each CD matures, you can reinvest the funds into a new CD with a longer term or withdraw the funds if needed.

This strategy can help you maximize your return on investment while still providing some flexibility in case you need access to your funds. By using a CD ladder for retirement savings, you can ensure that you have a steady income stream in retirement without taking on too much risk.

CDs are some of the most stable investments you can make. That said, they are usually used as an instrument to preserve wealth versus grow wealth. Therefore, I do not believe this is among the strongest options for those working towards financial freedom.

Bonds are a type of investment tool that can be used as part of a retirement investment portfolio. Bonds are essentially loans made to companies, municipalities, or governments, which are repaid with interest over a specified period of time.[xlix]

One of the primary advantages of bonds as a retirement investment tool is their relatively low risk compared to other investments, such as stocks. This makes them an attractive option for people approaching retirement and looking to preserve their capital.

There are several types of bonds available for retirement investors, including:

- **U.S. Treasury bonds:** These are issued by the U.S. government and are considered the safest type of bond investment. They offer a low rate of return but are virtually risk-free.
- **Municipal bonds:** These are issued by state and local governments to fund public projects. They are generally

exempt from federal taxes and may also be exempt from state and local taxes.

- **Corporate bonds:** These are issued by companies to raise funds for business purposes. They typically offer a higher rate of return than government bonds but also carry a higher level of risk.

Bonds can be purchased individually or through mutual funds or exchange-traded funds (ETFs) that invest in bonds. Bond funds can offer greater diversification and lower costs than buying individual bonds but may also carry some risk. Like CDs, bonds are usually purchased to preserve the money you already have. For me, I leave these to my grandparents.

Investing in precious metals, such as gold, silver, platinum, or palladium, can be a means to save for retirement. Precious metals are tangible assets that have been used as a store of value for centuries and are often seen as a hedge against inflation, economic uncertainty, or the apocalypse.

There are several ways to invest in precious metals, including:

- **Physical bullion:** Involves purchasing gold or silver bars or coins and storing them in a safe place, such as a safe deposit box. This can be a good option for those who want to have physical possession of their investment, but it also carries risks, such as theft or loss (e.g., government-contracted moving companies).

- **Exchange-traded funds (ETFs):** ETFs are a type of investment fund that tracks the price of a particular commodity, such as gold or silver. They are traded on stock exchanges, making them a convenient way to invest in precious metals without physically owning them.
- **Mutual funds:** Mutual funds can also be invested in precious metals, either by holding shares in mining companies or investing in ETFs that track the price of the metals.

Investing in precious metals can offer several benefits for retirement investors, including diversification of their investment portfolio and protection against inflation. In addition, precious metals often perform well during periods of economic instability, making them a good hedge against market volatility. I personally own a small amount of silver, but it is ultimately a novelty. Appreciation of metals will never outperform the returns you can expect from other investment vehicles like those described above.

Pro Tip: If you learned anything from this chapter, it's to do the easy stuff (TSP, Traditional/Roth IRAs). If you're a little more confident, you should consider expanding into real estate. It can make you a lot of money at a greater risk. Avoid the fads

(Crypto/NFTs) and keep the low earners (CDs, Bonds, precious metals) for your grandparents.

Money Pits

- Inaction. Doing nothing or overanalyzing (i.e., Analysis Paralysis) each individual investment you make, so you end up making no investments.
- Chasing the latest 'get rich' investment fad. This is a get-rich slow plan. You don't have to be in a hurry. Fads are very risky.
- FOMO. Jumping on an investment you know little to nothing about because you don't want to miss out.
- Chasing market trends. So, your stocks took a dump, but it doesn't mean you should rush to sell. Remember, buy low/sell high.
- Not routinely revisiting your investments. Your portfolio is like a garden. It needs some tending. Move money between investment vehicles to enhance winners and move on from losers.
- Cashing out early and paying penalties or capital gains tax.

16

Dating and Marriage

"Before you marry a person you should first make them use a computer with slow internet to see who they really are."

~ Will Ferrell

I know that Kanye West is a controversial figure and may not be the best example for those reading this book. Still, I must recognize his lyrical genius from 2005 when he recorded the song *Gold Digger*. In my opinion, Kanye created a lens through which people measure the true intentions of a potential partner.

Dating and marriage may be the biggest risk you take financially. This is not to scare anyone but rather to let you, the reader, know how vital it is to understand the complexities of dating and marriage in your financial life. So, while you are discussing the future with your long-term sweetie and before you go running to the chapel, take some time and talk through this chapter together. Doing so will put you both on solid footing.

Will you fight about money in your relationships? Yes. Will money be something that you will have to navigate as a couple, not once, but always? Yes. Will relationships become increasingly difficult when two people with limited financial literacy join their finances and debt into one giant mess? Absolutely. Does that mean you can't and shouldn't plan for financial success with your partner? No way.

This chapter is for the love birds in the room. As I said, this is a good one to share with each other and revisit often. The best relationships prioritize communication about the complicated so that both individuals understand and work towards common goals. Emotions can cloud discussions dealing with money. In an effort to avoid marriage counseling and still give you the tools to be successful in this area, the material will focus on the factual and logical. If you keep to the numbers and your shared financial goals, your joint financial future and your relationship will be better for it. Let's dive in.

Dating: Understand the signals you are throwing out when you go out. If you pay for everything while dating, you are setting an expectation. A better way to impress a potential partner is to demonstrate maturity and discuss your long-term financial goals and aspirations. Put it out early that you are looking for someone who shares your drive to escape the rat race and do what you are called to do rather than chase the highest salary. That sounds a lot sexier than, "I'd take you out to Chick-Fil-A today, but I blew my paycheck on bottle service last night." I'm not saying don't do the occasional extravagant things but make sure your partner understands that these are not the norm and that your priority is to achieve long-term wealth.

Marriage: Ensuring you are starting a marriage on the right foot will prevent finances from becoming the undoing of your relationship. As unromantic as it sounds, your relationship will be better for it. Then it would help if you discussed some specifics:

- **Credit Score:** Your credit score has a lot to do with what you are charged to borrow money. Both partners must know each other's credit score. Once you are legally married, any credit you apply for jointly will take the low of the two scores into consideration.
- **Debt:** Discuss any debt you or your partner may have, including student loans, credit card debt, car loans, and mortgages. Talk about your plans for paying off the debt and how it will impact your finances as a couple.
- **Income:** Be open about your income and how much you earn. Discuss your financial goals and how you plan to achieve them together.
- **Spending Habits:** Discuss your spending habits and any financial goals you may have as a couple. Talk about your

individual priorities when it comes to spending money, and work together to create a budget that reflects your shared values.

- **Joint or Separate Accounts:** Decide whether you want to have joint or separate bank accounts. Discuss the pros and cons of each option and decide what works best for your situation. I always recommend avoiding separate accounts for the first 1-3 years. This allows each individual to continue working towards ongoing financial goals while realizing the savings from newly shared expenses. This should be a come-up for you both.
- **Retirement Planning:** Discuss your retirement plans and how much you're currently saving for retirement. Talk about how you plan to achieve your retirement goals together.
- **Insurance:** Discuss any insurance policies you have, including health, life, and car insurance. Decide whether you want to combine policies or keep them separate.
- **Estate Planning:** Discuss your estate planning goals and any assets or debts you may have. Talk about how you plan to manage your estate together.
- **Double Income:** Can you survive on a single salary? Can you both work if you are planning on having children? Does your spouse have a career that is transferable as you move?

When you both feel like you are ready to move forward, be sure you don't get married until you can afford it. Overpaying for a wedding ceremony is not only a terrible use of your money, but it may also place your marriage at risk.

> *A 2014 study published in Social Science Research Network looked at the weddings and marriages of more than 3,000 people in the U.S. and found that the price of a wedding is likely to play into your chances of future separation. According to the study, recently married couples who spent more than $20,000 on their wedding were 46 percent more likely to split than those who spent around $5,000 to $10,000. And those who spent $10,000 to $20,000 were 29 percent more likely to get divorced than those who spent in that mid-range cost.*[l]
>
> *Spending less than this mid-range might also decrease your chances of splitting in the future. According to the study, married couples who spent just $1,000 or less on their wedding were 54 percent less likely to get divorced compared to those who spent around $5,000 and $10,000. And those who spent anywhere between $1,000 and $5,000 were 19 percent less likely to get divorced.*[li]

Unique to the military. Many military installations are in rural areas. With your paycheck and career, you can be seen as a way out of a small town. Watch for fast-moving relationships, especially if you are in technical training or at your first assignment.

Suppose you get married to a foreign national while stationed overseas. In that case, there are many additional financial considerations to consider, like the cost of permanent visas and/or the naturalization process. Additionally, you may become the primary breadwinner for your family because a lot of degrees/certifications (e.g., Doctor, Lawyer, Teacher, etc.) from overseas do not automatically transfer to the U.S. system.

Overall, getting married will have a financial impact on both parties involved. Therefore, it's important to carefully consider marriage's financial implications and communicate openly and honestly with your spouse about your financial goals and expectations. It may also be helpful to seek professional advice, such as from a financial planner or attorney, to help you navigate the financial aspects of marriage.

Money Pits

- Overspending on a wedding.
- Getting married before understanding your partner's financial goals and spending habits.
- Placing your assets together too early in a relationship.

17

Separation and Divorce

"And so rock bottom became the solid foundation on which I rebuilt my life."

~J.K. Rowling

This is a chapter that no one wants to arrive at, but many of us will need it. Separation and divorce can be the single biggest kick to your financial junk. This is the one time being in the military will not benefit you. Suppose you find yourself going through separation or divorce. In that case, you may be held financially responsible for two places to live, spousal maintenance, child support, and a division of all assets and debts.

We all have war stories or friends with the worst breakups in history. Recently, a friend of mine described their ongoing separation.

My bro has approximately eighteen years in and is now living on a friend's couch while continuing to pay the mortgage on a house that he can't visit. Lawyer fees insert an additional burden on an already financially stressed situation. He is coming up on retirement and is living off his credit cards.

Most people might think that financial literacy is something that all older people, or those of higher ranks, inherit at some point in their careers. This is a false assumption. Members of every grade and at every age going through separation or divorce can benefit from the information in this chapter. The goal by the end will be to have you on the road to financial recovery.

The divorce rate among U.S. Military is almost twice the national average.[lii] Anecdotally, this may be due to frequent moves, deployments, long hours, or secrecy required.

Divorce can have a significant financial impact on both parties involved. Some of the ways that divorce can affect someone financially include:

- **Loss of income:** If one spouse was financially dependent on the other, they might experience a loss of income after the divorce. This can make it difficult for them to cover their expenses and maintain their standard of living.
- **Division of assets:** In a divorce, assets such as property, investments, and retirement accounts may need to be divided between the two spouses. This can result in a loss of assets for one or both parties.

- **Legal fees:** Divorce can be costly, as it typically involves hiring attorneys and paying court fees. These costs can add up quickly and may strain one or both parties' financial resources.
- **Changes in living arrangements:** After a divorce, one spouse may need to move out of the family home, which can result in additional expenses such as rent or a mortgage payment.
- **Changes in insurance coverage:** After a divorce, one spouse may lose access to their ex-partner's insurance coverage, which can result in higher insurance premiums.
- **Changes in tax status:** Divorce can also have an impact on your tax situation, as you may need to file taxes as a single person rather than as a married couple. This can affect your tax rate and the amount of taxes you owe.

Overall, divorce can have a significant financial impact on both parties involved. Therefore, it's important to carefully consider the financial implications of divorce and seek professional advice, such as from an attorney or financial planner, to help you navigate the process.

Here are some steps you can take to recover financially from divorce:

- **Create a budget:** After a divorce, it's important to get a handle on your finances and create a budget to help you manage your expenses. This can help you see exactly where your money is going and identify areas where you may be able to cut back or save more.
- **Negotiate a fair settlement:** If you are going through a divorce, it's important to negotiate a fair settlement that considers both parties' assets and debts. This can help you protect your financial interests and ensure you have the resources you need to move forward.
- **Review your insurance coverage:** After a divorce, you may need to review your insurance coverage and make any necessary changes. This may include getting your own health insurance policy, changing your car insurance to reflect your new living situation, or updating your life insurance policy.
- **Consider your tax situation:** Divorce can affect your tax situation, as you may need to file taxes as a single person rather than as a married couple. Reviewing your tax situation with a tax professional to ensure you take advantage of all the credits and deductions you are entitled to is a good idea.
- **Build up your emergency fund:** After a divorce, it's important to have an emergency fund to help you cover unexpected expenses or a loss of income. Aim to save

enough money to cover three to six months' worth of living expenses.

- **Seek professional help:** If you are struggling to manage your finances after a divorce, it may be helpful to seek the advice of a financial planner or attorney. These profess-sionals can help you understand your options and create a plan to get your finances back on track.
- **Focus on the future:** It's natural to feel overwhelmed after a divorce, but it's important to try to focus on the future and take steps to rebuild your financial stability. This may include setting financial goals, making a budget, and working to improve your financial situation over time.

Different parenting arrangements can have a financial impact on both parents. Some ways that different parenting arrangements can affect you financially include:

- **Child support:** If you are the non-custodial parent (meaning you do not have primary physical custody of the child), you may be required to pay child support to the custodial parent to help cover the costs of raising the child. Child support payments can be a significant financial obligation and may impact your ability to meet your own expenses.

- **Shared expenses:** If you are the custodial parent, you may be responsible for paying a portion of your child's expenses, such as medical bills, childcare costs, and extracurricular activities. These costs can add up and may impact your financial situation.
- **Loss of income:** If you are the custodial parent and you have to reduce your work hours or take time off work to care for your child, you may experience a loss of income. This can affect your ability to meet your financial obligations and maintain your standard of living.
- **Changes in living arrangements:** Different parenting arrangements may require you to change your living situation, such as moving to a new home or changing your housing arrangement. These changes can result in additional expenses or a loss of assets.
- **Changes in insurance coverage:** Different parenting arrangements may also affect your child's insurance coverage. It is critical to make insurance arrangements for your children. One unforeseen illness or accident can make it even more difficult to recover financially following your divorce.

Overall, different parenting arrangements can have a financial impact on both parents. Therefore, it's important to carefully consider the financial implications of different parenting arrangements and seek professional advice, such as from an attorney or financial planner, to help you navigate the process.

Money Pits

- Liquidating all your assets to settle your divorce in cash. Doing this will destroy all progress you have made in saving for your financial future. Instead, make every attempt to divide assets and keep them in the asset category.
- Failing to pay child support. As a government employee, your wages are subject to garnishment. This means the money you owe will be taken from your check before you receive your pay. This limits your ability to make your own financial decisions.
- Overspending on the items you need to start over. At least one spouse will need a new place to live, including basic furnishings, cooking items, and children's accommodations (if applicable). Purchasing a new home or complete furniture sets is not the way to recover financially. The best thing to do is simplify your living expenses to the absolute bare minimum.
- Trying to save money by not hiring lawyer. This will always end up costing you more in the long run.

18

Transition

"There are far better things ahead than we ever leave behind."

~ C.S. Lewis

If you make it this deep into the book, you are in for a real treat. This is the first chapter in the book I consider myself an expert. I spend several hours every week as a mentor to Service Members who are going through the transition to civilian life. If you are transitioning soon, I'd love to hear from you. Contact me on LinkedIn, in/trevorcnolan or you can contact me using the contact forms on my websites, TrevorCNolan.com or MilitaryMightPublishing.com. Leaving the military doesn't have to be on your shoulders alone. Surround yourself with a team of Veterans or civilians that are where you want to be, and use them.

Financially speaking, when I prepared to transition from the military, I started nearly two years ahead of time. In that time, I paid off every bill I could, completed large projects on the house (using cash, not credit), and minimized all other spending. Since

I was retiring from the military, I wanted to know if I could live my current quality of life on my projected retirement pay. I then started lifestyle design. An excellent book on this subject is '*What Color is Your Parachute*,' by Richard Nelson Bolles. It wasn't until approximately six months out that I discovered my next chapter would be as an entrepreneur. Since then, I have worked to become financially solvent in my businesses and have expanded into additional offerings. I tell you all this to say, create a plan and move out, make adjustments along the way, and don't ever quit on yourself. The money will come, especially when you don't need it.

This chapter, like the others, is not all-inclusive for every transition plan. It will, however, aid you in the formulation and execution of a financial transition plan. This chapter works best when you implement it well before you need to. Everyone leaves the military: you get out, you retire, or you die. You might as well do it on your terms.

Changing careers can be exciting but also risky, especially if it means taking a pay cut or going back to school. Here are a few steps you can take to financially prepare for a career change:

- **SkillBridge:**[liii] Look into the DoD SkillBridge program. It provides an opportunity for service members to gain valuable civilian work experience through specific industry training, apprenticeships, or internships during the last 180 days of their service. In addition, SkillBridge connects service members with industry partners in real-world job experiences.

- **Create a budget:** Determine how much money you will need to cover your expenses during the transition period. This can help you identify any potential financial gaps and make a plan to bridge them.
- **Save money:** If you will be taking a pay cut or going back to school, saving as much money as possible can be helpful before making the switch. This can help you weather any financial challenges you may face during the transition.
- **Explore financing options:** If you will need to go back to school or pay for additional training, research free options for Veterans first before financing options such as student loans. Be sure to compare the terms and conditions of each option carefully.
- **Consider consulting or freelance work:** If you are able to do so, you may be able to supplement your income by taking on consulting or freelance work in your new field while you are making the transition.
- **Network and build connections:** Building connections in your new industry can be vital to finding job opportunities and getting your foot in the door. Network with professionals in your field, join relevant

organizations, and participate in industry events to build your network.

Determine what is important. If you retire, you can live on your retirement if you scale back your lifestyle.

What to do next

The average enlisted retirement is $30k-$35k per year, while the average officer retirement is $60-$70K per year.[liv] With TSP, you cannot start drawing it without a penalty until fifty-nine and a half years old. The median American full-time salary is $53,490.[lv] In the event you need to find a job to carry you over until retirement age, here are some options.

GS vs. Contractor vs. Civilian:

- **Government Service (GS):** GS jobs used to come with job security. That has changed with the recent furloughs, Reductions in Force (RIFs), and continuing resolution budgets. These positions come with less money than contractor jobs but with arguably better benefits. You can also potentially convert some of your active-duty years toward a GS retirement. There is a "cooling off" period of 180 days before you can take a GS position, so be prepared to take some time off or a temp position if you plan to go GS.[lvi]

- **Contractor:** Contractor jobs are a way to earn more money, especially if you have a security clearance. The tradeoff is job security. Contracts are constantly being recompeted. If your company loses a recompete, you will probably be picked up by the winning company, but it may affect your seniority (PTO, vesting, etc.). If you take a break and let your clearance lapse, you may have a more challenging time getting a contractor job. Consult the JAG before retiring and tell them what type of work you plan to do and which companies you are applying to in order to avoid a conflict-of-interest violation. Most government contractors provide a 401K retirement plan. If they offer contribution matching, always take it. This is when they will match your contributions to your retirement (usually as a percentage). It is essentially free money.
- **Civilian:** You have a unique set of skills. Not only have you been taught leadership, but you've also been given the opportunity to practice it. Companies often specifically seek out Veterans or those with prior military service to lead within their organizations.

Security Clearance: Your security clearance has value after you leave the military. The chart below shows the average salary based on what clearance you have. If you get out while your investigation/reinvestigation is ongoing, it will often not be adjudicated, and you will not have a clearance. I have seen people delay retirement until they had final adjudication in order to keep their clearance so they could land a high-paying contracting job.

Clearance	Value
Confidential	$83,041
Secret	$86,671
Top Secret	$107,148
Top Secret/SCI	$110,796

Value of a Security Clearance (CAO Aug 2022)[lvii]

What's most important: I recently listened to a group of active-duty members argue over what they believed was most important for getting a good job outside the military. The three camps were certifications, education, and experience. I made a point to stop them and have them consider another alternative. In my opinion, the most important thing you take into the civilian world is your reputation. When hiring, company managers will most often look up the candidate on LinkedIn and see who the candidate is connected to. Your connections say a lot about who you are. If you have a shared contact with the hiring manager, you can bet the company will reach out to that third party to find out more details about you. Your reputation will win or lose you opportunities.

Proof of Experience: Keep all your performance reports. These will serve as proof for anything that you put on your resume.

VA Disability Rating: Start your medical processing with the VA six months to the day before your retirement or separation. If you plan to go the BDD (Benefits Delivery at Discharge) route, you MUST submit your VA claim no later than 90 days PRIOR to your separation/retirement date. Once you are within 89 days, you are no longer eligible for the BDD program and will have to submit a "fully developed claim." Make sure any medical issues have been documented. Get copies of all of your medical records and make an appointment with the VA. Work with a Veteran service organization that can help you file a claim, like Wounded Warrior Project or DAV. Never pay for this service. They will help you scrub your records for anything they think will contribute to your disability rating. By starting early, you should get your rating before you retire, and if applicable, disability payments will begin on your retirement or separation date. You may wait six to twelve months to get your rating if you still need to. You will get back pay, but it is better to get it upfront.

Money Pits and Bad Decisions

- Allowing yourself to accept a low salary because you have your retirement and/or VA disability pay. Never undervalue yourself. Shoot as high as possible upon separation/retirement, as it sets the lower limit for the rest of your life. If you take a $60k job when you should be getting $90k, how long will it take you to get there? By the time you get to $90k from $60k, how much, further along, would you be had you initially started at $90k? This is the biggest mistake I see transitioning members make.

- Not investing in your civilian self while still on active duty. I know it's hard to believe, your unit will go on without you. No, you are not working on something that only you can accomplish. Use the time you need to successfully transition.
- Having a bad resume or no resume. You should always have one up to date and tailor it to the position you are applying for. A bad resume demonstrates that you are not worthy of high pay and responsibility.
- Selling back leave when you retire. It makes more financial sense to receive your full military pay and pay from your new civilian job during your terminal leave period. This practice, called double-dipping, is a great way to get a large sum of money as you depart the military. Be careful, this influx of money will affect your income taxes. Don't blow the money just because you have it.
- Separating or retiring while your security clearance reinvestigation is in progress. This will potentially cost you hundreds of thousands in future income.

19

More Money Pits and Bad Decisions

"I have been exceptionally good at making bad decisions all my life. Fortunately, bad decisions make great stories."

~ Debi Tolbert Duggar

This is one of my absolute favorite chapters in the book. Mainly because it lets me put everyone on blast for spending all their money on the dumbest of dumb shit; think of this chapter as the Darwin Awards for financial decisions. For those that don't know what a Darwin Award[lviii] is, it's an international honor awarded to people who die from something spectacular, usually of their own bad decision. An example might be building and testing your own bungee cords off a suspension bridge or fighting a lion armed only with your white-belt achievements in taekwondo. In both of those examples and many others found online, the awardees (victims) are always missing knowledge and discipline.

Trigger warning, if you feel like you are being personally attacked while reading this chapter, please do not lash out at me for your terrible life choices. You have already made a real improvement by reading this book and putting its recommendations into practice. But unfortunately, if you already went out and bought yourself a pet tortoise that will live the next 80 years, you are stuck with the thousands of dollars that thing will eat over its lifetime. So, financially speaking, it's probably best to see if the zoo will take her.

Have fun with this one and don't be the one to sabotage your financial future.

The most expensive items that people routinely spend money on varies depending on individual circumstances and priorities. However, some common expenses that tend to be significant for many people include:

- **Food:** The cost of food, including groceries and dining out, can be a significant expense for many people. Learn to cook and buy generic/store-brand products to save even more money.
- **Clothing:** Clothing costs, including the cost of buying new clothing and maintaining and repairing existing clothing, can be a significant expense for some people.

- **Entertainment:** The cost of entertainment, such as going to the movies, concerts, or sporting events, can be hugely expensive, especially because tickets are often purchased from secondary markets well above face value.
- **Rebuying everything at every new assignment:** Yes, I'm looking at you. Unfortunately, this is a trap so many military people run into. When looking for a place to live for your next assignment, pick the place that fits what you already own.
- **Keeping up with the Joneses:** This is the "Everyone else is doing it" fallacy. It's human nature to want to fit in. The easiest (and most superficial) way is to dress, drive, and live like everyone else. I argue that doing so will lead to superficial relationships and empty bank accounts.
- **Lending or borrowing money:** When you joined the military, someone in your life probably saw you as a person they could borrow money from. Only lend money you can afford to lose. If you must borrow money, make sure you have a plan to pay it back and do so as soon as possible.
- **Speeding/Parking tickets:** These are expenses you can control. This is just throwing money away. Let off the gas, lead foot.
- **DUI:** The ramifications to your career and bank account far outweigh the cost of a ride home. Always have a plan to get home safely. If you get a DUI on base, you will lose

your base driving privilege for a year. Imagine having a coworker pick you up from the gate every day for work.

- **Drugs:** This should go without saying. Don't smoke crack or anything else, for that matter. When you get caught, your career will be over and your earning potential on the outside will be significantly reduced. Should you fall into addiction, chances are you will lose everything. You'll need more than this book to get right.
- **Interest/Late Fees:** Blockbuster made a substantial portion of its income (16%) from late fees before it went under.[lix] If you are too young to know what Blockbuster was, Google it. The same applies to no-interest/same-as-cash loans with a set payoff date. You will be required to pay all interest from the inception of the charges and possibly late fees for the entire length of the loan. So, once again, only get into a contract that you have a plan to pay off on time.
- **Hidden Fees:** Everywhere you look, there seem to be more and more fees. Hotels have resort and parking fees. Concert tickets cost almost twice the face value. Ensure you know the actual and total cost before signing any agreement.
- **Gambling:** The house <u>always</u> wins.
- **Collectibles:** Their value is inversely proportional to their rarity. The bottom line is if a lot of folks are collecting it, their value is less. There is also a high chance

they get damaged, destroyed, or go missing on your next move.

- **Losing your Security Clearance:** Due to non-reporting or false reporting. This can be absolutely devastating to your earning potential.
- **Boats and RVs:** Unless you are going to use them often, it is cheaper to rent them when you need them. Along those lines, Outdoor Recreation often rents them both.
- **Too Good to Be True Offers:** Be wary of any offer that does not give you time to think/research.
- **PT Tests Failures:** Face it, the PT test is not exceptionally hard. However, you can make it more difficult on yourself if you only work out once a year during the test. Failure puts you on your leadership's radar, not in a good way. A failure could lead to consequences that could prevent promotion. Promotion equals more money in your pocket. Don't jeopardize it over a PT test. Continued failures could lead to a discharge. That would seriously impact you financially.

20

Bonus: How to Cut Back without Feeling Deprived

"It's not having what you want, it's wanting what you've got."

~ Sheryl Crow

In my completely unscientific opinion, when you pack on a few extra pounds, there are only a few ways to trim down, eat less or exercise more. The worst part of cutting weight is that it always corresponds with the holidays, family cookouts, your birthday, Superbowl, or a work trip to Vegas. It sucks being the person hanging out near the store-bought veggie tray while everyone else is enjoying all the good food. Your finances follow a very similar pattern. If you want to turn the tides on your finances, you either cut spending or generate additional revenue.

What if I told you, you could have your favorite foods while still moving in the right direction? Too good to be true? Actually, not in this case. This chapter will explore my favorite ways to cut back without feeling like the one holding the veggie tray. Instead, think of these as my personal life hacks for financial freedom. So, while all those silly civilians are spending big bucks to 'enjoy' life, you will be rewarded with deeper happiness and money in the bank.

It has always surprised me how few people look to do free or low-cost social events first rather than big-ticket social outings. The military offers some great experiences for free or at a low cost. These could include trips and tours, outdoor adventure trips, or intramurals. To some, it seems more noble or ballin' to make it rain wherever you go. But, let's be honest, no military member is taking home that much money. The ideas provided in this chapter are just a few of the thousands of things you could do to improve your quality of life without feeling financially deprived.

- **Host a Game Night Extravaganza:** Instead of spending money at a bar or club, invite your friends over for a game night. Choose from classic board games like Monopoly or Scrabble or try something newer like Cards Against Humanity or Settlers of Catan. Get creative and make it a themed event like "Medieval Night" or "Superhero Night." And remember the snacks!
- **Channel Your Inner Picasso:** Instead of buying expensive art, create your own masterpieces! Grab some paint and a canvas, and let your inner artist run wild. And if your painting doesn't turn out as expected, call it "modern art."

- **Find Hidden Gems in Your City:** It's common for military members to be stationed in different locations worldwide, providing opportunities to explore new places and experience different cultures. Take a walk or bike ride around the local area, visit local landmarks and museums, or try new foods at local restaurants.
- **Start a Book Club:** Instead of buying new books, start a book club with your friends. Choose a book, read it, and discuss it over coffee, tea, or beer. Bonus points if you dress up as your favorite character from the book!
- **Take Advantage of Free Trials:** Many subscription services offer free trials, so take advantage of them! Binge-watch your favorite shows, listen to new music, or learn a new skill, then ghost them before you get charged.
- **Get Creative with Gifts:** Instead of buying expensive gifts, get creative and make your own! For example, create a personalized photo album filled with gym selfies, bake some homemade cookies, or write a heartfelt letter to your parents. The thought and effort you put into the gift will be more valuable than the price tag.
- **Get Involved in Intramural Sports:** Many military installations offer intramural sports leagues for Military Members to participate in. For example, join a softball or basketball league or try your hand at something new like kickboxing or martial arts.
- **Join a Fitness Group:** Joining a fitness group can be a great way to stay active and meet new people. Many

installations have running or cycling clubs, yoga classes, or CrossFit groups that are free or low-cost.

- **Volunteer in the Community:** You can positively impact their community by volunteering your time and talents. For example, volunteer at a local animal shelter, participate in community cleanup, or mentor local youth.
- **Organize a Potluck or BBQ:** Organize a potluck or BBQ with friends. Everyone can bring a dish or beverage to share, and you can enjoy some good food and company without breaking the bank.
- **Go for a Hike or Bike Ride:** Explore the great outdoors by going for a hike or bike ride on a local trail. Most trails are free to access and provide stunning views of nature.
- **Take Advantage of Military Discounts:** Many businesses offer military discounts, so be sure to take advantage of them. Military members can save money from movie theaters to amusement parks while still having fun.

There are plenty of fun and inexpensive ways you can spend time without spending your last dollar every month. However, staying on a budget doesn't mean you have to sacrifice fun and adventure. With a bit of creativity and a sense of humor, you can enjoy life to the fullest without breaking the bank.

21

Resources

"Take the time to vet the source before you make it a resource."

~ Loren Weisman

Army Air Force Mutual Aid Association (AAFMAA): Life Insurance, Wealth Management and Mortgages. https://www.aafmaa.com/

Department of Veteran Affairs: Access and manage your VA benefits and health care. https://www.va.gov/

Disabled American Veterans (DAV): A non-profit organization that provides VA Benefit help, Medical Transportation, Employment & Entrepreneurship and Transition services. https://www.dav.org/

Military.com is a website that provides news and information about the United States military, Service Members, Veterans, and their families, as well as foreign policy and broader national security issues.

Military One Source from the Department of Defense is your 24/7 gateway to trusted information, resources and confidential help. When MilLife happens, it's your "first line of support" — giving Service Members and military families tools to stay well and thrive. https://www.militaryonesource.mil/

USA.GOV: Get info about military benefits like health care, housing, and education. Discover programs that help with military life, like job search help for spouses and dealing with deployments—access free family counseling. Get tax filing help geared for the military.

US Department of Defense: Resources. https:// www. Defense .gov/Resources/

VA Loans: https://www.benefits.va.gov/homeloans/

Wounded Warrior Project: A non-profit organization that provides post 9-11 Veterans programs in mental health, career counseling, long-term rehabilitative care, and VA advocacy. https://www.woundedwarriorproject.org/

Biography

Trevor C. Nolan is a retired U.S. Air Force Veteran and a Latino business leader who founded Military Might Publishing in 2023. He holds the distinction of being an Adelante Leadership Institute Fellow and a Center for Creative Leadership Lideramos Fellow. As the CEO of Summit Advanced Program Consulting, Trevor supports veteran-owned businesses and advocates for social action.

In addition to his business endeavors, Trevor is an active executive member of the El Paso County (Colorado) Salvation Army Advisory Board and serves as a DoD SkillBridge Mentor. His first book, *Military Money: How to Thrive on a Government Salary*, is the first in a series of books aimed at helping Service Members and their families navigate and thrive in the military.

Trevor's second book, *The Penguin That Wanted to Be a Seal*, is a children's book that teaches military children that no goal is too great. It is scheduled for release Fall 2023, and all net proceeds will be shared between the Special Operations Warrior Foundation (https://specialops.org/) and the Navy SEAL Foundation (https://www.navysealfoundation.org/).

To learn more about the Military Might series or to share your own story, visit militarymightpublishing.com.

Contact me:

Websites - TrevorCNolan.com
MilitaryMightPublishing.com
LinkedIn - /company/military-might-publishing/
Facebook - @MilitaryMightPublish
Instagram - @MilitaryMightPublishing

Military Might Publishing is a proud member of the Independent Book Publishers Association.

ENDNOTES

---

[i] Forrest, Conner (23 October 2018). "These 10 college majors have created more billionaires than any other fields of study". TechRepublic, 23 Oct. 2018, https://www.techrepublic.com/article/these-10-college-majors-have-created-more-billionaires-than-any-other-fields-of-study/

[ii] Mcleod, Saul. "Maslow's Hierarchy of Needs Theory." Simply Psychology - Study Guides for Psychology Students, Simply Psychology, 2 Mar. 2023, https://simplypsychology.org/maslow.html.

[iii] FtDeVault, Janine. "Average Apartment Size in the United States: The Complete Guide - Flex: Pay Rent On Your Own Schedule." Flex, 3 June 2022, https://getflex.com/blog/average-apartment-size/.

[iv] Ft"Townhouse." Missing Middle Housing, 24 Sept. 2020, https://missingmiddlehousing.com/types/townhouse.

[v] Araj, Victoria. "What Is the Average Square Footage of a House?" What Is The Average Square Footage Of A House? | Rocket Mortgage, 27 Feb. 2023, https://www.rocketmortgage .com/learn/average-square-ootage-of-a-house.

[vi] "Loans." HUD.gov / U.S. Department of Housing and Urban Development (HUD), 20 Sept. 2017, https://www.hud.gov/buying/loans.

[vii] "Debt-to-Income Ratio: How to Calculate Your DTI." Edited by Kim Lowe, NerdWallet, 23 Feb. 2023, https://www.nerdwallet.com/article/loans/personal-loans/calculate-debt-income-ratio.

[viii] "A Quick Comparison of FHA and Conventional Loans." Fahe, 23 July 2019, https://fahe.org/fha-vs-conventional-loans/?gclid=Cj0KCQjwwt

WgBhDhARIsAEMcxeAmsfiCH5FlNAdOV_5hzorrPeZGXc46m8c9_QKOb5nUllNoccITjXAaAkEkEALw_wcB.

[ix] "What Is a Loan-to-Value Ratio and How Does It Relate to My Costs?" Consumer Financial Protection Bureau, 9 Sept. 2020, https://www.consumerfinance.gov/ask-cfpb/what-is-a-loan-to-value-ratio-and-how-does-it-relate-to-my-costs-en-121/.

[x] "A Quick Comparison of FHA and Conventional Loans." Fahe, 23 July 2019, https://fahe.org/fha-vs-conventional-loans/?gclid=Cj0KCQjwwtWgBhDhARIsAEMcxeAmsfiCH5FlNAdOV_5hzorrPeZGXc46m8c9_QKOb5nUllNoccITjXAaAkEkEALw_wcB.

[xi] Christian, Rachel. "Here's How Making 1 Extra Mortgage Payment Could Shave Years off Your Debt." The Penny Hoarder, The Penny Hoarder, 19 Dec. 2022, https://www.thepennyhoarder.com/debt/one-extra-mortgage-payment-a-year.

[xii] "Cutting Pet Care Costs." ASPCA, 2021, https://www.aspca.org/pet-care/general-pet-care/cutting-pet-care-costs.

[xiii] "Cutting Pet Care Costs." ASPCA, 2021, https://www.aspca.org/pet-care/general-pet-care/cutting-pet-care-costs.

[xiv] "How Much Is Pet Insurance in 2023?" Forbes, Forbes Magazine, 21 Mar. 2023, https://www.forbes.com/advisor/pet-insurance/pet-insurance-cost/.

[xv] "Servicemembers' Group Life Insurance (SGLI)." Veterans Affairs, 1 Mar. 2023, https://www.va.gov/life-insurance/options-eligibility/sgli/.

[xvi] Veterans' Group Life Insurance (VGLI)." Veterans Affairs, 1 Mar. 2023, https://www.va.gov/life-insurance/options-eligibility/vgli/.

[xvii] Zander, Jeff. “Term vs. Whole Life Insurance: What's the Difference?” Ramsey Solutions, 3 Feb. 2023, https://www.ramseysolutions.com /insurance/term-life-vs-whole-life-insurance.

[xviii] “Umbrella Insurance - How It Works & What It Covers.” GEICO, https://www.geico.com/information/aboutinsurance/umbrella/.

[xix] Konish, Lorie. “This Is the Real Reason Most Americans File for Bankruptcy.” CNBC, CNBC, 11 Feb. 2019, https://www.cnbc.com/2019/02/11/this-is-the-real-reason-most-americans-file-or-bankruptcy.html#:~:text=And%20for%20many%20Americans%20who,or%20time%20out%20of%20work.

[xx] Hayes, Adam. “Power of Attorney (PoA): Meaning, Types, and How and Why to Set One Up.” Investopedia, Investopedia, 22 Nov. 2022, https://www.investopedia.com/terms/p/powerofattorney.asp.

[xxi] “Armed Forces Vacation Club - Official AFVC Website.” Armed Forces Vacation Club - Official AFVC Website, https://www.afvclub.com/.

[xxii] “Thrift Savings Plan (TSP).” MyArmyBenefits, https://myarmybenefits. us.army.mil/Benefit-Library/Federal-Benefits/Thrift- Savings-Plan-(TSP)#:~:text=If%20you%20are%20a%20member,balance%20of%20your%20TSP%20account%2C.

[xxiii] “Retirement Savings Contributions Savers Credit: Internal Revenue Service.” Retirement Savings Contributions Savers Credit | Internal Revenue Service, 21 Dec. 2022, https://www.irs.gov/retirement-plans/plan-participant-employee/retirement-savings-contributions-savers-credit.

[xxiv] Orem , Tina, and Sabrina Parys. “2022-2023 Capital Gains Tax Rates & Calculator.” NerdWallet, NerdWallet, 16 Feb. 2023, https://www.nerdwallet.com/article/taxes/capital-gains-tax-rates#

[xxv] “MSRRA: Military Spouses Residency Relief Act.” Military OneSource, 14 Nov. 2022, https://www.militaryonesource.mil/financial-legal/legal/military-spouses-residency-relief-act/.

[xxvi] Lw. “Tax Payment: Which States Have No Income Tax.” MARCA, Marca, 5 Feb. 2023, https://www.marca.com/en/lifestyle/us-news/personal-finance/2023/02/05/63dfcff2e2704ef1028b458c.html

[xxvii] Published by Statista Research Department. “Median Household Income by Education U.S. 2021.” Statista, 11 Oct. 2022, https://www.statista. com/statistics/233301/median-household-income-in-the-united-states-by-education/.

[xxviii] “Loans.” HUD.gov / U.S. Department of Housing and Urban Development (HUD), 20 Sept. 2017, https://www.hud.gov/buying/loans.

[xxix] “MSRRA: Military Spouses Residency Relief Act.” Military OneSource, 14 Nov. 2022, https://www.militaryonesource.mil/financial-legal/legal/military-spouses-residency-relief-act/.

[xxx] “Dantes - College Credit by Examination.” DoD VoIEd Programs, DANTES, https://dantes.doded.mil/EducationPrograms/get-credit /creditexam.html.

[xxxi] Mulnik, Faustina. “8 Reasons Why Bilingual Employees Get Paid More.” Homeschool Spanish Academy, 10 Sept. 2021, https://www.spanish. academy/blog/8-reasons-why-bilingual-employees-get-paid-more/.

[xxxii] "About GI Bill Benefits." Veterans Affairs, 14 Feb. 2023, https://www.va.gov/education/about-gi-bill-benefits/.
[xxxiii] "DoD Cool Portal - Homepage." Office of the Secretary of Defense, 15 Mar. 2023, https://cool.osd.mil/.
[xxxiv] "Home." TRICARE, 1 Dec. 2022, https://www.tricare.mil/Plans/HealthPlans.
[xxxv] Steel Supplements. "What Is the Average Cost of a Gym Membership?" Steel Supplements, 12 July 2021, https://steelsupplements.com/blogs/steel-blog/what-is-the-average-cost-of-a-gym-membership.
[xxxvi]"Cutting Pet Care Costs." ASPCA, 2021, https://www.aspca.org/pet-care/general-pet-care/cutting-pet-care-costs.
[xxxvii] "Antivirus Home Use Program (AV HUP)." Home Use Program, https://www.usmcu.edu/IT-ET-Group/Helpdesk/Home-Use-Program/.
[xxxviii] "How to Set Your Freelance Editing Rates." Reedsy, 23 Jan. 2019, https://blog.reedsy.com/freelancer/how-to-set-your-freelance-editing-rates/.
[xxxix] "Pay Yourself First: What It Means and How to Do It." Capital One, Capital One, 14 Mar. 2023, https://www.capitalone.com/learn-grow/money-management/pay-yourself-first/.
[xl] "Debt Management Guide." Investopedia, Investopedia, 24 Feb. 2023, https://www.investopedia.com/articles/pf/12/good-debt-bad-debt.asp.
[xli] "What Is a Home Equity Line of Credit and How Does It Work?" Bank of America, https://www.bankofamerica.com/mortgage/learn/what-is-a-home-equity-line-of-credit/.

[xlii] "How to Maintain a Good Credit Score." Capital One, Capital One, 19 Jan. 2021, https://www.capitalone.com/learn-grow/money-management/how-to-maintain-good-credit-score/.
[xliii] Thrift Savings Plan, https://www.tsp.gov/.
[xliv] Lake, Rebecca. "Retirement Saving and Investing for Military Personnel." Investopedia, Investopedia, 2 Feb. 2023, https://www.investopedia.com/retirement-saving-and-investing-for-military-personnel-5193117.
[xlv] Absher, Jim. "The Blended Retirement System Explained." Military.com, 19 Dec. 2022, https://www.military.com/benefits/military-pay/blended-retirement-system.html.
[xlvi] "Individual Retirement Accounts (IRAS)." Individual Retirement Accounts (IRAs) | Investor.gov, https://www.investor.gov/additional-resources/retirement-toolkit/self-directed-plans-individual-retirement-accounts-iras.
[xlvii] Kastrenakes, Jacob. "Beeple Sold an NFT for $69 Million." The Verge, The Verge, 11 Mar. 2021, https://www.theverge.com/2021/3/11/22325054/beeple-christies-nft-sale-cost-everydays-69-million.
[xlviii] . "Certificates of Deposit (CDS)." Certificates of Deposit (CDs) Investor.gov, https://www.investor.gov/introduction-investing/investing-basics/investment-products/certificates-deposit-cds#:
[xlix] Fernando, Jason. "Bond: Financial Meaning with Examples and How They Are Priced." Investopedia, Investopedia, 9 Mar. 2023, https://www.investopedia.com/terms/b/bond.asp.
[l] Kurtzleben, Danielle. "What Causes Failed Marriages: Poor Communication, Incompatibility…and Big Engagement Rings?" Vox, Vox, 15 Oct. 2014,

https://www.vox.com/2014/10/15/6978187/what-causes-failed-marriages-poor-communication-incompatibility-and.

[li] "If You Did This at Your Wedding, You're More Likely to Get Divorced." Yahoo!, Yahoo!, 1 Dec. 2021, https://www.yahoo.com/video/did-wedding-youre-more-likely-213048903.html.

[lii] "Military Members Have Highest Divorce Rate of Any Profession." Miller Law Firm, 15 Sept. 2022, https://www.millerlawfirmtn.com/blog/2022/04/military-members-have-highest-divorce-rate-of-any-profession/.

[liii] "What Is SkillBridge?" DOD SkillBridge - What Is SkillBridge?, 24 Mar. 2023, https://skillbridge.osd.mil/program-overview.htm.

[liv] Hartman, Rachel. "How Much Will I Receive When I Retire from the Military?" US News & World Report, 9 Dec. 2022, https://money.usnews.com/money/retirement/baby-boomers/articles/how-much-will-i-receive-when-i-retire-from-the-military.

[lv] Cristiano, Brittany. "This Is the Average US Salary for 2023 & These Jobs Pay so Much More." Narcity, Narcity, 21 Feb. 2023, https://www.narcity.com/average-us-salary-2023-jobs-pay-much-more.

[lvi] "Job Seekers." U.S. Office of Personnel Management, https://www.fedshirevets.gov/job-seekers/things-you-should-know.

[lvii] Jillian Hamilton / Aug. "Survey Results Show a Top Secret Clearance Can Earn Higher Compensation." ClearanceJobs, 18 Aug. 2022, https://news.clearancejobs.com/2022/08/18/survey-results-show-a-top-secret-clearance-can-earn-higher-compensation/.

[lviii] Northcutt, Wendy 'Darwin'. "The Darwin Awards!" Darwin Awards: Evolution In Action, https://darwinawards.com/.
[lix] McKinnon, Tricia. "8 Reasons Why Blockbuster Failed & Filed for Bankruptcy." Indigo9 Digital Inc., Indigo9 Digital Inc., 11 Jan. 2023,
https://www.indigo9digital.com/blog/blockbusterfailure.

Made in the USA
Monee, IL
06 July 2023